ORIGAMI AND PAPERCRAFT

A STEP-BY-STEP GUIDE

PAUL JACKSON AND VIVIEN FRANK

THE APPLE PRESS

A QUINTET BOOK

Published by Apple Press Ltd.
6 Blundell Street
London N7 9BH

ISBN 1-85076-140-X
Reprinted 1989

This book was designed and produced by
Quintet Publishing Limited
6 Blundell Street
London N7 9BH

Art Director: Peter Bridgewater
Designer: Linda Henley
Editors: Sandy Shepherd, Judith Simons
Photographer: Andrew Sydenham
Stylists: Paul Jackson, Vivien Frank
Illustrator: Lorraine Harrison

Typeset in Great Britain by
Central Southern Typesetters, Eastbourne
Manufactured in Hong Kong by
Regent Publishing Services Limited
Printed in Hong Kong by
South Sea International Press Limited

ACKNOWLEDGEMENTS

The authors and publishers would like to thank the following companies for their generosity in supplying the materials used for the craftwork throughout this book: Compton Marbling, Falkiner Fine Papers, J Hewitt & Sons, Paperchase, Wiggins Teape Ltd, S F Williams (Foils) Ltd, Winsor & Newton. They would also like to thank the British Paper and Board Industry Federation for information, Jessica Dodd and Sue Matthews for invaluable assistance, Andrea Lyttleton for all calligraphy, Maureen Richardson for papermaking suggestions and June Tunmore for the paper flowers.

CONTENTS

INTRODUCTION

Paper is one of Man's greatest inventions. Think how many times a day you use it as writing paper, wallpaper, tissues, banknotes, newspapers, books, magazines, envelopes, packaging, tickets, photographs, cheques, computer print-outs – the list is almost endless.

Think also of how many times a day you throw paper away. That list too is almost endless. The truth is that we do not always think about paper. We see it as a short-lasting, everyday material to be used and discarded. But think again!

For arts and crafts, paper is the most versatile of all materials. There are thousands of different papers in an enormous range of colours, weights and textures. Paper is readily available, usually inexpensive, simple to store and requires the help of only the most basic materials and equipment, such as scissors or glue, to transform it into any number of beautiful objects. Sometimes, as in origami, only the paper itself is used.

What's more, the variety of papercrafts is such that whether you like to make things that are decorative, practical, ingenious, geometric or expressive, there is bound to be one craft that will appeal to you.

The projects inside have been chosen to show the diversity of papercrafts. They are divided loosely into two sections: the first shows how you can give a sheet of paper an interesting surface, either by making your own paper or by decorating existing sheets; the second introduces some three-dimensional papercrafts, such as serviette folding, papier mâché, pop-ups, boxes and bags, or paper flowers.

We, the authors, hope that our enthusiasm for all things paper will inspire you to make some of the projects, and that they will give you pleasure and satisfaction.

Paul Jackson

Vivien Frank

PAPER AND EQUIPMENT

Page 7 Top Crêpe and double crêpe papers are forms of tissue paper which have been passed through a patterned roller when wet; this gives them their characteristic crinkled and stretchy qualities.

Page 7 Bottom Textured papers. The texture is printed on and gives a soft looking, rich surface, although not as vibrant as patterned papers.

There are three types of paper: handmade, mouldmade and machinemade and paper has two basic and important qualities – weight and grain. Handmade papers, which often incorporate long fibres, have no grain (the direction in which the fibres lie) and have four deckle edges (a deckle is the rough edge of the paper). Mouldmade papers are less expensive than handmade ones and are made by machine, but have two deckle edges and longer fibres than those used in machinemade papers. Mouldmade and machinemade papers both have a grain.

Other terms which are often used when talking about paper are 'laid', 'wove' and 'sized'. 'Laid' paper is made on a mould which has wire, or sometimes wooden, bars laid across the frame. These bars allow a thinner deposit of pulp to be laid and leave an impression in the sheet of paper. This impression may be visible only against the light. Watermarks are formed in the same way. Paper without these lines is called 'wove', from the woven mesh on which the pulp is poured. Paper can be 'sized', which means that it is coated with a glue substance (usually gelatine or starch), or it can be 'unsized'. Sized paper is less absorbent than unsized and therefore ink or paint do not bleed when drawn or painted on it. Unsized paper is known as 'waterleaf'.

PAPER WEIGHT

Paper is often measured by grammes per square metre, referred to as g/m^2 or gsm^2. Where the weight of paper is given in pounds, it refers to pounds per ream (a ream is 500 sheets, whatever the sheet dimensions). It is possible to convert pounds per ream to grammes per square metre but it is rarely necessary.

An average paper, such as writing paper, weighs between 80 and 120 gsm^2. Tissue and Japanese papers are obviously much lighter. Paper weighing more than 225 gsm^2 is card; it becomes board when it weighs 500 gsm^2 and more. To complicate matters further, card and board are also measured in micrometres, which indicates their thickness.

Bottom left Decorated origami and gift-wrapping papers are printed as part of their manufacturing process. Some are printed on one side only, which increases their versatility in papercrafts.

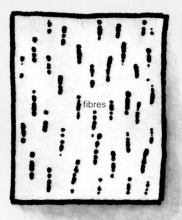

1 A sheet of paper with the grain running from top to bottom.

2 The sheet will bend easily when the lefthand edge is brought over to the right, because the bend follows the direction of the grain.

3 The sheet will not bend as easily when the top edge is brought down to the bottom, because the bend runs across the direction of the grain.

4 A torn edge is straighter when it follows the direction of the grain than when it runs across the grain.

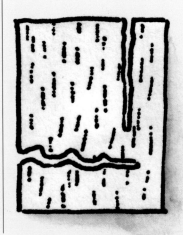

PAPER GRAIN

The grain of paper is pronounced in machinemade papers because the mould on which they are made is a moving belt and the fibres settle in the direction of the movement of the belt. This grain can be used to advantage in that paper will fold, curve, tear and crease more easily along its grain. But it also has disadvantages: when wetted, as in glueing, the fibres swell widthways but not lengthways, and although they compress again when dry, if two surfaces are being joined, you may end up with a curved surface. To avoid this, try dampening both sheets of paper.

To find out which way the grain runs in a piece of paper, curl the paper in both directions and, while pressing gently with one hand, feel which way bends more easily. Another way, although somewhat extravagant, is to tear two strips from the paper, one in each direction. When you are tearing with the grain, the tear will be much cleaner and less irregular. There is also grain in card and board; discover this by flexing the sheet between your hands and then turning it through 90° and flexing it the other way; it will flex more readily in the direction of the grain.

Below Lightweight card has many uses, from making templates to small boxes. Heavier card and corrugated paper can be used for packaging or surface decoration.

Right Foil papers are made by coating paper with adhesive and then with coloured metal powders, which are then burnished. Embossing is often applied to metallic foils backed with paper, as here. This is done by running paper between rollers which have been engraved with a pattern.

Above Ingres (or Strathmore) papers are often recognizable from their uneven surface appearance with visible hair-like fibres. They are lightweight to mediumweight papers.

Left Gift-wrap papers come in a huge range of patterns and textures and are printed onto white paper. The reverse is left unprinted. They are invaluable when decorative effects are needed.

Left Japanese papers are often extremely fine in appearance, but because they are made with long fibres, they are usually very strong.

Right Coloured papers and card come in a wide range of weights and colours and are an attractive alternative or contrast to white.

Below Handmade papers are the most beautiful of all papers. Their surfaces are rich in colour and texture and will make any papercrafts project look extra special.

Above Marbled papers are formed by laying coloured oil-based inks onto water. Paper is laid on top and then removed, pulling the inks with it. The best examples are marbled by hand, although cheaper printed sheets can also be purchased.

CRAFT EQUIPMENT

1 Felt-tipped pens
2 45° triangle
3 Small plastic ruler
4 'M'-shaped safety ruler
5 Metal cutting ruler
6 Automatic feed pencil
7 Graphite pencils
8 Clear adhesive tape
9 Pencil sharpener
10 Glue stick
11 Clear adhesive
12 PVA adhesive
13 Round-tipped craft scissors
14 Retractable craft knife with snap-off blade
15 Double-sided adhesive tape
16 Scissors
17 Vinyl eraser
18 Self-healing cutting mat

MAKING PAPER

For most of its 2,000-year history, paper has been made by hand. However, since the Industrial Revolution in the late 18th century and the invention of machinery that could mass-produce paper, the craft has become a highly sophisticated industrial science. Yet making paper is essentially a simple process and one which is tremendous fun and surprisingly creative. It is a craft in which all the family can participate – even young children can make their own sheets of paper.

Traditionally, handmade paper is made from hemp or, more commonly, from recycled cotton rags. Both substances have unusually long fibres, which bind together well in the papermaking process to form a strong material. To make these fibres into paper they have to be broken down and separated, which means boiling them in caustic substances. To keep the method practical enough for you to try in your own kitchen, this chapter will deal only with recycling existing papers. Quite a few books have been written in recent years which explain how to make paper from plant fibres, so if you get the bug, look for them in your local library or bookshop.

Left Here are just a few examples of the many effects of colour, texture and design that guarantee making paper at home is such fun.

SUITABLE PAPERS FOR RECYCLING

The best papers for making good white sheets include unprinted computer paper, typing paper, writing paper and photocopier paper. Other good, but more unusual, papers include Ingres (Strathmore) paper (all weights), cartridge or drawing paper, watercolour paper, card, printed computer paper and old novels or picture books printed on good-quality paper. Even tissues, serviettes and tea bags can be used. To help soften thicker papers and card, soak them overnight before blending them (see below).

Avoid using newspapers: they are made from cheap, poor-quality pulp which has a high acid content and turns brown very quickly. Also, avoid shiny papers such as china paper and glossy magazine paper: they are coated with china clay, which turns to a crumbly powder when recycled. Poster paper and other papers coated with a coloured pigment should also not be used. If in doubt, always try out a paper. In truth, very few types are unsuitable for recyling.

MOULD-AND-DECKLE METHOD

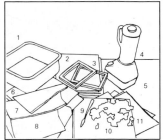

EQUIPMENT

1 Large oblong bowl
2 Two wooden boards **3** Two wooden frames (see page 18) **4** Blender
5 Plastic sheeting
6 Large format newspapers
7 Curtain netting (see page 18) **8** Old bath towel **9** Palette knife
10 Viscose kitchen cleaning cloths
11 Paper for recycling

This method makes thick sheets of paper because the deckle frame traps a lot of pulp on top of the mould. For thinner sheets, add extra water to the pulp.

EQUIPMENT

■ Paper to be recycled.
■ A blender. One with a 2 pint/1 litre/4 cup capacity jug is the best, but any size will do. Paper is not poisonous, so rest assured that the jug will not be contaminated.
■ At least one large, oblong mashing-up bowl. Circular or oval ones are the wrong shape. Make sure they are very clean, or unwanted particles of dirt will appear in the paper pulp.
■ An old bath towel to cut up, capillary matting (available from plant nurseries) or any other very absorbent material.
■ Smooth, all-purpose, striped viscose kitchen cleaning

cloths (you will need one for each sheet of paper). Don't use coarse cloths because they texture the paper when it is pressed, unless, of course, you want this texture.
■ Plenty of clean newspaper, preferably broadsheet (large format), which has not been folded into quarters. If possible, start collecting well ahead of making paper because you will need a lot.
■ Two sturdy wooden boards about 12 × 18 in (30 × 46 cm). The boards need not be identical or clean, but the wood must be strong enough not to bend, so don't use hardboard (Masonite) or thin plywood.
■ A palette knife.
■ A few heavy books or other weighty objects.
■ A large flat surface to work on.
■ Plastic sheeting, refuse bags or a waterproof tablecloth to cover the work surface and nearby carpets.
■ A sink.

MAKING A MOULD AND DECKLE

You will need a mould and deckle on which to deposit the wet pulp before it is pressed and dried to become paper. They can be bought in craft shops or by mail from craft suppliers, but it is easy enough to make your own. If you have enough materials, it is well worth making a few sets of moulds and deckles.

EQUIPMENT

■ Enough ¾ in (2 cm) square wood to cut four 8 in (20 cm) lengths and four 5 in (12.5 cm) lengths
■ Plain curtain netting or similar open-weave fabric. The size of the mesh is not critical, but should not be too tight or too open
■ Drawing pins (thumb tacks)
■ Eight 'L'-shaped brass plates (with screws), not wider than the wood
■ A screwdriver

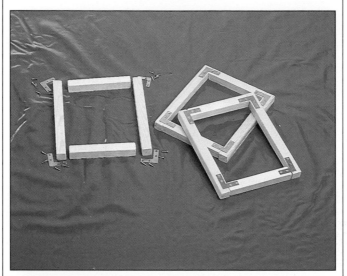

1 Cut the wood to the lengths described above, and arrange them to make two identical frames. Let the ends of the short lengths touch the sides of the long lengths. Screw the brass plates to the corners of one face only, to hold the frames together. Alternatively, if you have the equipment and necessary carpentry skills, mitre the corners, apply a waterproof adhesive and nail them together.

2 Pin the curtain netting over the top face of one frame. A constant tension of net is important, so first pin it to the middle of one outside edge, then to the middle of the opposite outside edge, pulling it reasonably tight. Pin the middles of the two remaining outside edges, then begin to work towards the corners, pulling the net reasonably tight and pinning it as you go.

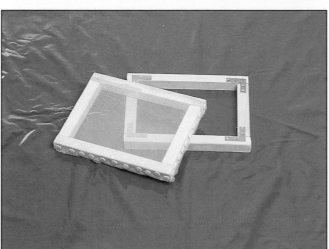

3 To complete, fold over the net at the corners to make a neat finish. Trim off the excess net. This frame is the mould, and the uncovered one the deckle. The mould and deckle can be made much larger, but you will not be able to use them in a bowl. A baby bath is a good alternative.

PREPARING THE PULP

The pulp can be prepared in advance and can be done by young children who greatly enjoy ripping paper to shreds! Tear several layers of paper at once to speed the process.

1 Tear (never cut) the paper to be recycled into pieces about the size of large postage stamps. Fill the blender no more than three-quarters full of water and put in no more than 35 torn pieces of paper for every 2 pints/1 litre/4 cups of water. Switch the blender on.

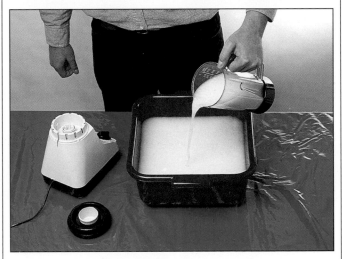

2 Pour the pulp into the washing-up bowl. Repeat the blending process until the bowl is half to two-thirds full, but not brimming over.

BLENDING TIMES

As a rough guide, blend computer, photocopy, typing, writing and similar papers for 25–35 seconds, cartridge (drawing) paper and Ingres (or Strathmore) papers for 40–50 seconds, tissue for 60 seconds and card for 70–90 seconds (less if previously soaked overnight in water). The result should be a thin fibrous soup. If globules of fibre are still coagulating, blend for a little longer. If the machine is labouring, take out some of the paper. Do not be tempted to overload the jug.

FORMING THE SHEET

Stir the pulp gently with your hand to distribute the fibres evenly in the water. Unstirred, they soon settle to the bottom. Repeat this every time the pulp is left to stand for more than a few minutes. This agitation is an important part of the process: be careful not to forget it as it will affect the success of this project.

1 Fit the deckle exactly over the mould, so that the brass plates on the deckle are on the top surface away from the mould, and the net on the mould rests against the deckle in the middle of the 'sandwich'.

2 Hold the long edges of the mould and deckle together tightly at the far end of the bowl, making sure that the deckle is facing you.

3 Then, with smooth movements, lower the short edges of the mould and deckle vertically into the pulp.

4 Pull the mould and deckle towards you while at the same time bringing them to a horizontal position under the pulp, with the deckle on top of the mould.

5 Lift the mould and deckle straight out of the pulp, being careful to keep them horizontal. Hold them a few inches above the pulp and let the excess water drain through, at the same time shaking them gently backwards and forwards, left and right, to help the fibres settle evenly on the net as the water drains.

6 Rest two adjacent edges of the mould on the nearside corner of the bowl.

7 Support the underside of the mould with one hand, and with the other, lift off the deckle quickly. Be careful not to drag the deckle into the pulp on the net, or it will damage the edge of the paper. Also avoid letting water drip off the deckle onto the pulp.

8 The pulp is now ready for couching.

COUCHING

This is a traditional term for transferring wet pulp from the mould onto the sheet of material on which it will dry. Before forming the sheet of wet pulp on the mould, prepare a couching mound. Make this from an old bath towel which has been cut up, capillary matting, or other very absorbent material.

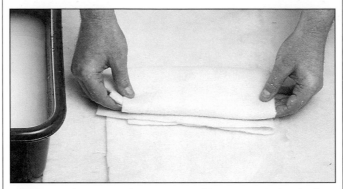

1 Cut up the material to make a small mound the same shape and size as the mould. Wet it to help it lie flat. (Take some time to do this properly.)

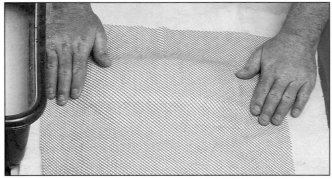

2 Cover the mound with a damp, all-purpose, striped viscose kitchen cleaning cloth, so that the nearside short edge of the cloth just covers the nearside edge of the mound.

3 To form the wet pulp on the mound, rest the long edge of the mould on the cloth 1 in (2.5 cm) in front of the foot of the mound, so that the pulp is on the far side of the mould, facing the mound. Hold as shown.

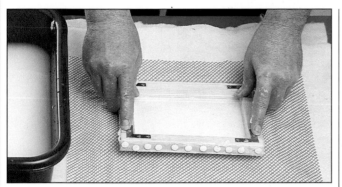

4 In as fluent a movement as possible, lower the sides of the mould gradually onto the mound, pressing firmly.

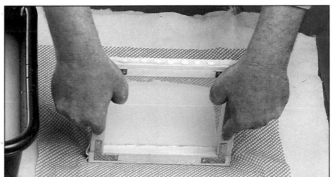

5 Lift the bottom edge off the cloth, pushing the top edge firmly into the cloth.

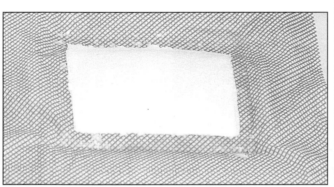

6 The pulp should stick to the cloth. If it doesn't, this is probably because the mound is too tall, too flat or has the wrong dimensions. Experiment with its shape until the pulp couches satisfactorily. Alternatively, the cloth may be too dry; wet it again.

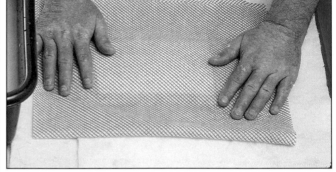

7 Fold the remainder of the cloth over the sheet of pulp. Be very careful not to leave any creases in the cloth where it covers the pulp, or they will be moulded into the sheet when it is pressed, spoiling its smooth surface.

8 Lay a second damp cloth over the first and couch another sheet onto it as described above. Fold the cloth in half as before.

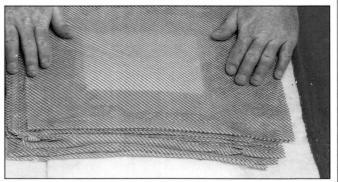

9 The process can be repeated a dozen times or more, each new sheet being couched on top of the others in a growing pile. Don't forget to lay out a new damp cloth for every sheet so that each is in its own folded cloth 'sandwich'.

PRESSING

The method described here looks very rough and ready (it is!), but works extremely well. A more professional way would be to use a proper paper press. They are, however, quite expensive and difficult to find.

1 Put the pile of couched sheets onto one half of the back page of a broadsheet (large format) newspaper. Fold the other half of the newspaper over the pile, sandwiching the sheets in the middle.

2 Put the sandwich between two sturdy wooden boards.

3 Stand on the boards for about two minutes, squeezing out most of the water from the cloths. The heavier you are the better. This is best done out of doors, because a surprising amount of water will come out. Alternatively, do it on a bathroom floor or other tiled floor which can be mopped dry.

CAUTION!!

Unless you have a waste-disposal unit, when you empty the bowl of pulp at the end of a paper-making session, do not pour it down a sink. The fibres will congeal in the sump, causing a blockage. Instead, sieve the pulp through a strainer so that the water drains into the sink. Put the dough-like pulp that has remained in the sieve into the dustbin, or use it to make a deckle-only sheet of paper (see below).

DRYING

This is the stage which is easiest to rush, but you must be patient. Let the paper dry at its own pace. Attempts to speed the process by ironing the paper or placing it near a heater may 'cockle' (warp) it.

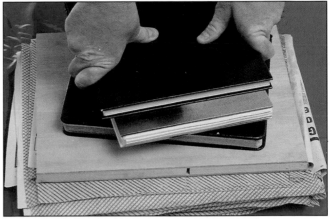

1 Remove the pile of damp cloths from the sodden newspaper. Take a new, dry newspaper and turn over three sheets to pages six and seven. Lay out two cloths on page six, then turn over three more sheets, covering the cloths, and lay out two more cloths on page twelve. Repeat the process until the newspaper is full. Turn to the back page and fold the newspaper in half from top to bottom across the middle. Repeat with other newspapers until all the cloths have been laid into them.

2 Put the newspapers back between the boards and weight them with a few large books or other objects of a similar weight.

After about two hours, remove the cloths from the newspapers and lay them out as before into fresh newspapers. Once again weight them between the boards and leave for a few hours. Repeat the laying-out process every six hours or so until the cloths and the handmade paper are completely dry. This may take a day or more, depending on how thick the paper is and how much water it held originally.

3 When the paper is completely dry, open the cloths and gently slip a palette knife under the edge of the paper. Move it slowly under the sheet all round in a sequence of slicing movements, separating the paper delicately from the cloth. It is possible to do this with an ordinary kitchen knife, but a palette knife is easier to use and kinder to the paper, particularly if it is thin.

4 Hold an edge of the paper and peel off the cloth. Do not hold the cloth and pull the paper off because this will bend the paper and possibly damage it. The paper is now finished (**right**).

OTHER METHODS

THE MOULD-ONLY METHOD

The mould-and-deckle method but without the deckle will produce a thinner sheet because the absence of a deckle means that less pulp is held on the mould.

▌ Use the mould without the deckle to produce finer sheets. If the pulp is already watery, the sheets formed using this process will be extremely thin and beautifully delicate.

SIZING

This process is necessary to stop inks and paints from bleeding into paper when they are written or drawn on. Unsized paper acts like blotting paper, diffusing a line of colour, though this can sometimes be an attractive effect.

To size a sheet, simply add two teaspoons of coldwater starch to the bowl of pulp. Stir it and carry on making the paper as before. If you want a smooth writing surface, press the sheets with a medium-cool iron when they are nearly dry. Never iron the paper directly, but do it through a layer of fabric.

THE DECKLE-ONLY METHOD

This is a rough-and-ready method for making paper, or at least a fibrous mat, without the need for a net stretched over the deckle.

▌1 Blend the pulp for about one-third longer than the usual time, then pour it through a sieve. The water will drain away to leave a thick dough-like pulp trapped in the sieve.

▌2 Lay out a damp kitchen cloth and place a deckle onto one half of it. Empty the contents of the sieve into the frame and spread it about evenly to make a pulp mat. Sieve as much pulp as is needed to form a mat ¼-½ inch (6-12 mm) thick. If you have a pipette or turkey baster to hand, squirt some thin pulp onto the mat to help it bind.

▌3 Remove the deckle and fold the remainder of the cloth over the pulp. Press and dry as described for the mould-and-deckle method.

CREATIVE EFFECTS

SPECKLED SHEETS

1 Make a bowl of white pulp. Blend a small quantity of orange paper in a little water for about 10 seconds, so that it is not quite pulped, but shredded into small speckled pieces, and pour it into the white pulp.

2 Repeat the previous step with a similar quantity of grey paper.

3 Form the sheet on the mould as before (with or without a deckle), then couch, press and dry. The sheet will be white with orange and grey speckles.

You may think, and with reason, that it is a little odd to tear up a piece of paper, only to reconstitute it so that it looks pretty much the same at the end as it did at the beginning!

If these are your thoughts, look at the following creative suggestions. It is at this point that papermaking becomes an open-ended art form, where the only limitation is your imagination. Assume no rules, no right or wrong, just enjoy it. You will be surprised how often a silly idea, or indeed a silly mistake, can give a beautiful result.

4 Try speckling the paper with white speckles in a coloured pulp, or with any other combination of colours. As an alternative, blend tea leaves in a little water and add them to a white or coloured pulp. You could also add small objects directly to the pulp without blending them: seeds, short lengths of hair or coloured threads, confetti, small scraps of fabric, colourful flower petals or autumn leaves, all make an attractive effect when embedded in the paper.

LAID-ON EFFECTS

1 Couch a white sheet. Then tear up strips or cut out shapes from sheets of coloured tissue paper and lay them on top of the couched sheet. As the sheet dries, the tissue will remain stuck to it.

2 To achieve subtle coloured effects try the following method. Couch a sheet and lay tissue paper, thicker paper, wool, or whatever you choose on top. Form another sheet using the mould only and couch it exactly over the top of the first sheet. This traps the coloured items between two layers of pulp, but they will still be visible, if only faintly.

TIP

Try creating laid on effects with thin and thick pieces of coloured paper. With thick pieces, press and dry the paper on the couched sheets, then peel it off. Some of its coloured pigment will have run off onto the main sheet to form a coloured shadow (*see* left). Other interesting laid-on effects can be created with tickets, wool, petals, leaves (*see* left), sand, etc.

SHAPED PULPS

1 Couch a white sheet and mix a bowl of coloured pulp. Hold an edge of the mould (without the deckle) and drag part of it vertically through the pulp, net side first.

2 Remove the mould from the pulp – the pulp will be deposited onto only part of the mould. Couch it over the top of the white sheet.

3 The coloured pulp will cover part of the white pulp. Press and dry as before. Various effects can be achieved (**below**).

TIPS

■ Try mixing up a few differently coloured pulps and couching them on the same sheet, or dragging a corner of the mould through the pulp, in order to change the shape of the pulp on the mould.

■ To achieve more complex shapes of coloured pulp, stick a paper shape to the top of the net, leaving holes where the pulp has to couch. Put all the mould under the pulp in the conventional manner. Pull it out and remove the paper shape, taking part of the pulp with it. Those parts of the net that were not covered with the paper will have retained pulp. Couch onto a previously couched sheet.

USES FOR HANDMADE PAPERS

Plain white sheets or sheets of a pale colour make very attractive writing paper. For thin writing paper, form the sheets on a mould without a deckle, see page 26. If you do not want the writing inks to run, remember to size the pulp, see page 26. Thicker sheets make unusual business cards, calling cards, gift tags or table place names. To form the small shapes needed for business cards, either make a very small mould and deckle, see page 18, or mask part of a larger mould with a paper shape, see page 29.

Left To make greetings cards, glue a sheet of your paper to the front of an ordinary piece of card which has already been folded down the middle. Another sheet of handmade paper, possibly plain and starched, can be glued inside the card to hold a written greeting. Perhaps the most effective use of creative papers is to assemble a patchwork of sheets and frame them. Sheets which may be considered not good enough to become greetings cards or which are too eccentric, become surprisingly attractive as a patchwork. Framed, they are always a talking point.

DECORATING PAPER

There is an infinite number of ways to decorate paper, some of which will be explained in this chapter. Within each method there are many variations, because the results will differ depending on the type and colour of paper used. For example, ink on tissue paper will give a very strong colour, but if you thin the ink and splatter it on a heavy, absorbent, coloured paper the effect will be much more subtle.

Some of the techniques discussed will produce finished work, and others are only a step towards a bigger project. Just the basics of each method have been explained, but hopefully your imagination will be stimulated to experiment and take them further.

WEAVING

Paper weaving can be extremely challenging but can also be very simple. It can be used in a purely decorative way to make a picture or in a more practical way to form a box. The pleasure comes in the many exciting types and colours of paper you choose to use for your efforts. The main thing to remember is that there are no rules and the experimenting is all part of the fun. The paper used can be coloured, patterned or textured, and even illustrations from magazines.

EQUIPMENT

■ Various mediumweight papers
■ Adhesive tape
■ Glue stick
■ Scissors or craft knife
■ Metal ruler
■ Pencil

1 Using a metal ruler and a craft knife, cut strips of paper. These will provide straight edges in the pattern. Use a variety of colours, if desired.

2 Alternatively, tear strips to create a looser-edged pattern. Use different colours for greater effect.

3 When you are combining strips of paper in a woven design, the vertical strips represent the 'warp' threads and the horizontal strips the 'weft' threads, as in any form of weaving. Cut the warp into zigzags and thread different coloured and textured strips through it.

4 Alternatively, cut the warp into curves for a wavy pattern and thread different-coloured weft strips through it.

5 For a more random effect, tear the strips and lay them across and through each other. The warp can be spread out and the weft can be woven irregularly so that spaces show between the strips.

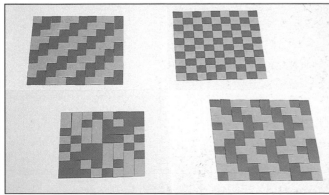

Above Rigid, geometric patterns are produced with straight-edged strips.

Right Create interesting patterns with irregular warp and weft strips.

COLLAGE

The word collage comes from the French verb *'coller'*, meaning 'to stick'. Collage is regarded as an art form and the examples shown here can be developed further.

1 Tear up small pieces of tissue paper and place on glued lightweight paper, using spray adhesive or a glue stick.

2 Leave some edges of the tissue paper unattached and allow them to overlap a little. Finished sheets can be cut up and used on the front of a greetings card, see pages 104 and 105.

Above These finished examples can be used for many of the projects covered later in the book.

STENCILLING

EQUIPMENT

■ Mediumweight paper
■ Stencil paper
■ Self-adhesive shapes
■ Foil
■ Spray diffuser
■ Toothbrush
■ Stencil brush
■ Sponge
■ Paint brush
■ Paints and paint palette
■ Coloured inks, felt-tipped pens and coloured pencils

Stencilling can be messy, so it is advisable to protect the working area and surrounding surfaces with newspaper to avoid accidents. The patterns in this section are mostly created by blocking out an area of paper and colouring the remaining part. The blocking out can be done using several kinds of stencils.

Above Cut shapes out from stencil paper. Both the negative and positive parts of the stencil can be used.

Left and below Fold a sheet of paper and cut or tear shapes out of the folded edges. Colour through or round the shapes onto another piece of paper.

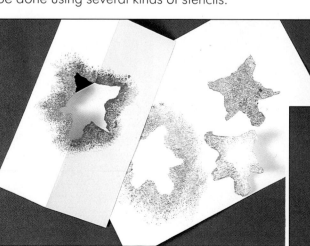

■ Try using self-adhesive shapes as stencils. Paint over them and then remove when dry.

■ Cut shapes out of a folded sheet of foil. Unfold the shape and brush one colour through it. Swivel the stencil round slightly and paint through it with another colour to create an attractive kaleidoscopic effect.

■ You can apply colour in a number of ways. Try brushing the colour on with an ordinary paint brush, or for a more stippled texture, use a stencil brush.

■ If you apply the colour with a sponge, some of the cellular texture of the sponge will transfer onto the paper. For an even effect, use a spray can or airbrush. For a fine stippled effect splatter the paint onto the paper from a toothbrush or a larger brush. Dip the brush in the liquid paint and shake off the excess before drawing a finger or ruler across the bristles. Keep the bristles facing downwards!

1 Using a leaf-shaped positive stencil, paint is applied to a coloured background with a sponge.

2 Using the cut-out leaf shape as a negative stencil, paint around the shape with a stencil brush.

3 You can have great fun experimenting with these methods. Try using several colours in one design, or use coloured paper as the background, as this will add to the design.

STENCILLING TIPS

■ Spray the paper with water first before you stencil onto it, to increase its absorbency; the colours will spread more when you apply the paint.

■ Do not make the paint too wet or it will run under the edge of the stencil.

■ Do not load too much colouring medium on the brush or sponge, or the texture of the mark will be lost.

■ Folded paper stencils cannot be used too often because they absorb the paint and become too sodden to be used cleanly.

■ When using self-adhesive shapes, allow them to dry before you remove them to make sure that you do not smudge any part of the design.

■ Try using acetate as a stencil material, and cut it with a scalpel or craft knife. As it does not tear, this material allows for quite a lot of detail and also has the advantage of being transparent so it can be positioned exactly with ease.

■ Try tearing a large shape from a piece of paper and place it on another sheet; paint over the edges all around the shape. Lift off and tear off the painted edge, making the shape smaller and changing it slightly. Reposition it within the painted area and, perhaps with another colour, paint over the new edge. Repeat the same process as many times as possible.

Above These examples were all created using the methods explained in this section.

RESIST METHODS

EQUIPMENT

- Wax crayons
- Wallpaper paste
- Wax candles
- Poster (alkyd) paints
- Bowl
- Wide brush
- Black drawing ink
- Mediumweight to heavyweight paper

These methods can be tightly controlled or very random. They can be done with wax crayons and paint, wax rubbings and paint, paste and paint, or wax crayons and ink. Wax crayons and paint and wax rubbings and paint are very similar in application, although the final result is very different in that the first can be used to create a picture, whereas the second produces a pattern. Paste and paint is not strictly a resist method, but the end result looks similar to other resist methods. It is a good way of making textured patterns on paper.

WAX RUBBINGS AND PAINT

1 Cover a textured surface, such as a strip of plastic netting, with a piece of white or coloured mediumweight paper and rub a candle or coloured wax crayon over the paper. Remove it from the textured surface.

2 Next, brush some thin water-based paint over the entire sheet. The paint can be one colour or can be brushed on in stripes of different colours.

3 Make sure that you brush the paint right over the edges of the paper, and protect the surrounding area with waste paper. Allow the paper to dry naturally.

Left These examples show a variety of rubbings on papers of different textures. Look around you for different materials which can be used for rubbings: cane chair seats, tennis raquets, brick walls, tree bark — the list is endless.

PASTE AND PAINT

1 Mix wallpaper paste to the directions on the packet – it should be reasonably thick but not lumpy. Add water-based paint to this mixture. Test the intensity of the colour on a piece of paper (**top**). Using a broad brush, spread the paste mixture across the whole sheet as evenly as possible (**above**).

2 Now let your imagination take over. Using a finger, the handle of a paint brush or an improvised comb (as above), draw patterns in the paste and paint mixture.

3 If you do not like the design, simply brush over it and start again! Depending on the amount of paste you use, the patterned paper will take quite a while to dry. To create a lighter appearance, when the paper is almost dry, lay a piece of thin paper (newsprint or similar) on top of the pasted paper and rub evenly over it, or use a roller, and then peel it off.

Right An infinite range of attractive designs can be created using different implements to pattern the paste mixture.

WAX CRAYONS AND INK

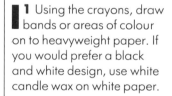

1 Using the crayons, draw bands or areas of colour on to heavyweight paper. If you would prefer a black and white design, use white candle wax on white paper.

Now, paint over the entire area with black drawing ink. It may be necessary to repeat this step in order to cover the wax crayon completely.

2 When the ink is dry, take any improvised drawing tool – the handle of a paint brush, the bottom of a pencil (**above**), an empty ballpoint pen or the end of a ruler

(**top**) – and scratch through the ink to reveal the colours of the crayons. Either draw a picture or make a pattern; whichever you choose the results will be stunning.

TIP

The above process can be reversed – paint an area with black paint, and when it is dry, colour in areas over it with the wax crayons, pressing firmly onto the paint. Then scratch through the wax areas to reveal black lines or shapes, giving more detail to the crayoned design. This method creates a more individual design than the wax band of colour painted with ink.

Left The two finished examples here show both random and controlled techniques.

DIPPING AND FOLDING

EQUIPMENT

▓ Thin absorbent
paper
▓ Kitchen tissue
▓ Small dishes
▓ Coloured ink, food
colouring or
watercolour paint
▓ Stiff brush
▓ Bulldog clips
▓ Roller

This method is simple, quick, colourful and, for these reasons, very exciting. It involves folding paper in various ways and then dipping it into a coloured liquid.

It is essential that you use very lightweight paper for this process, but you will have to experiment with different brands to discover which papers work best. For the photographed examples here, coloured tissue papers and large sheets of lens tissue, available in some specialist paper shops, have been used. Many of the tissue papers sold in packets are not colour-fast, and when they are wet their colour may run. This can add to the design, but you should be aware of this possibility. It may be advisable to wear surgical rubber gloves while working with your chosen colouring medium (household gloves are too cumbersome to enable you to unfold the wet tissue without tearing it).

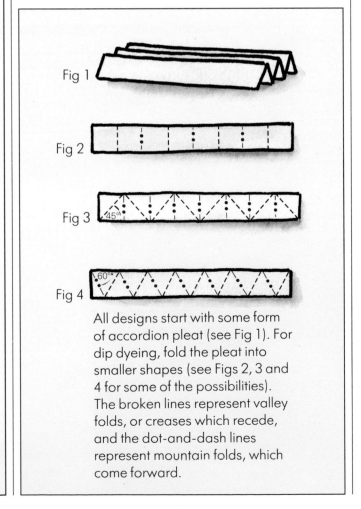

Fig 1

Fig 2

Fig 3

Fig 4

All designs start with some form of accordion pleat (see Fig 1). For dip dyeing, fold the pleat into smaller shapes (see Figs 2, 3 and 4 for some of the possibilities). The broken lines represent valley folds, or creases which recede, and the dot-and-dash lines represent mountain folds, which come forward.

1 Make an accordion pleat (see Fig 1) with your chosen lightweight paper – coloured tissue paper is ideal. Now fold as in Fig 2, 3 or 4, or experiment with your own folding ideas.

2 Pour some colouring – liquid watercolour, coloured ink, food colouring or similar – into a shallow container (preferably one that will not stain) and dip either a corner or an edge of the folded paper into it. Allow the paper to absorb the colour and let it spread a little.

3 Squeeze the excess liquid from the paper between kitchen tissue or newsprint. Continue to colour the folded paper as much as you require. At this stage the wet tissue is very fragile.

4 Unfold the paper so that it forms a long pleated strip. Place this strip on some waste paper, cover it with more waste paper and either rub hard all along the strip or, preferably, use a roller. This removes a great deal of the excess moisture.

TIPS

■ For softer-edged effects first dip the paper into water and squeeze it out before colouring it.
■ Be careful not to transfer any colour to the base of the iron; this is more likely to happen if the paper is still wet.

5 Now unfold the paper completely. Take care not to tear the tissue. Move the paper as little as possible at this stage and allow it to dry. When it is dry it can be ironed to remove some of the crease marks.

Below These dip-dyed examples show a variety of methods: use of wetted paper (left); felt pen technique (top right); wetted paper completely dyed (right); and use of dry paper (bottom right).

ALTERNATIVES

It is also possible to draw patterns into the folded shapes, using felt-tipped pens. When the paper has been folded, dip it in water and squeeze it gently so that it is damp, not dripping. The felt pens will now easily penetrate several layers of paper. Open the folds partially to check how far through the layers the colour has seeped, and rework the pattern from the faintest layer outwards. Fat felt tips give bold results, whereas fine felt tips give delicate and more detailed patterns. Dry as for the basic method already described.

Below right These finished examples show different ways of pleating: straight pleating of coloured tissue paper (left); diagonal pleating (top right); and repleating (bottom right).

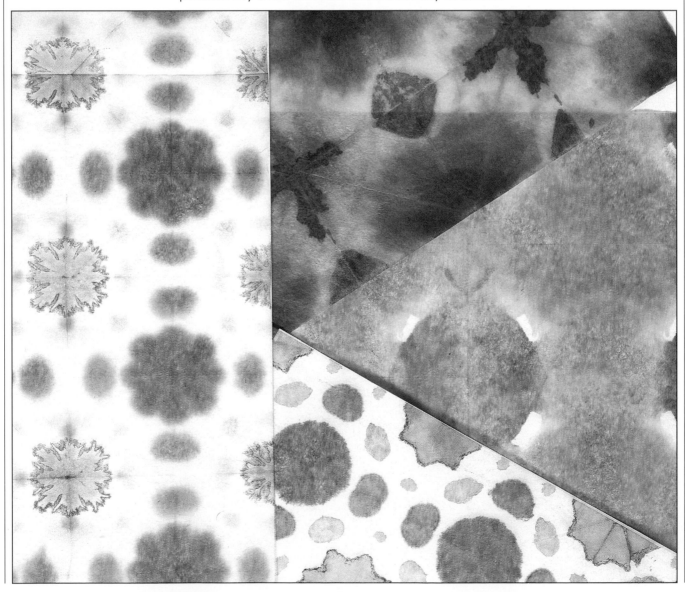

PLEATING

A method related to folding and dyeing is pleating and painting. There are many ways to pleat a piece of paper (see Figs 5–8 for some ideas). When the paper is pleated, hold the edges together on one side with bulldog clips, and paint the edges on the other side (see Fig 9). Repeat the process for the opposite edges. Dry as for the basic method. It is possible to repleat another design – checks or chevrons, for example – when the paper has dried, and to paint it again.

The finished papers are extremely decorative and can be used for many other projects: greetings cards, see pages 104–5; wrapping gifts, see pages 88–9; papier mâché decoration, see pages 54–6. The tissue paper can be mounted onto other sheets of paper using spray adhesive. It could be used in this form for lining envelopes, see page 106, and as a cover for a stationery holder, see pages 109–14 or a notepad.

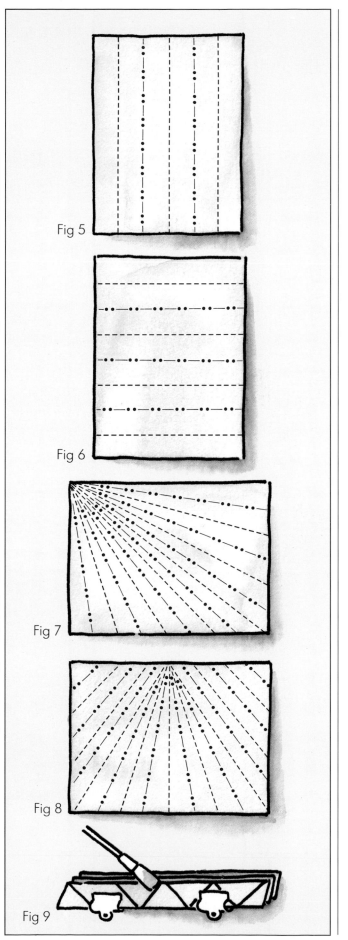

Fig 5

Fig 6

Fig 7

Fig 8

Fig 9

MARBLING

EQUIPMENT

- Shallow tray (photographer's tray or roasting tin)
- Wallpaper paste and mixing bowl
- Oil colours
- Turpentine or white spirit (mineral spirit)
- Ox-gall (available from artists' supply stores)
- Jars for colours
- Old newspapers
- Sticks or knitting needles, for stirring
- Medicine dropper or pipette
- Card
- Double-sided adhesive tape
- Ruler
- Pencil
- Pins

The technique of marbling, by which paper is given a marbled pattern, is thought to have been invented in eastern Europe in the sixteenth century. The process relies on the fact that oil and water do not mix. Oil colours are floated on size or water, the paper is laid on the surface of the liquid, and when it is lifted off, picks up the pattern of the colours. It is a simple technique but needs practice to achieve consistent patterns. However, do not be deterred because it is a most enjoyable craft to practise, and even your first experiments will be presentable.

Marbled papers are mainly associated with bookbinding, but these days they appear on many household accessories: lamps and lampshades, candlesticks, wastepaper bins, stationery holders and boxes, etc. Some marbled papers are now printed, but these do not usually have the quality – both visually and texturally – of handmade ones.

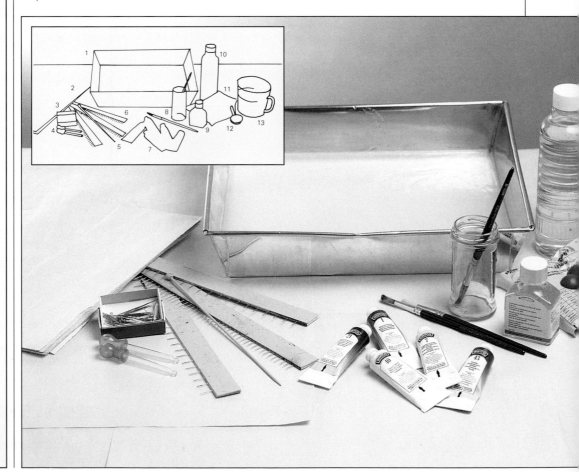

PREPARING THE BATH

Using approximately one heaped tablespoon to 2 pints/ 1 litre/4 cups of hand-hot water, mix about one-quarter of the water with the paste (also known as size) in the tray until the paste is smooth. Then add the rest of the water, stirring well so that the size is free of lumps. Allow the mixture to stand for a while and prepare the colours.

Marbling can be done with a single colour, particularly if you are using coloured paper, but two or three colours can also be used. Squeeze out some oil paint onto a saucer or a palette. Add some turpentine or white spirit (mineral spirit) and stir continuously until the colours are thinned to a runny consistency. Then transfer the colours to individual jars.

The next step is the most uncertain part of the process and will probably require several attempts. Add ox-gall to the colours in order to reduce the surface tension and to allow the colours to spread on the size. Ox-gall reacts differently with each colour, depending on factors such as the temperature of the room and the size, the consistency of the colours, etc. Start by adding five drops of ox-gall to two teaspoons of each colour. If colours are being placed on top of each other, the second colour will need additional ox-gall. However, you can make these adjustments during the marbling session.

Make sure that you have plenty of strips of newspaper or newsprint prepared for skimming excess colour from the surface of the size. The strips should be slightly narrower than the tray and 3 in (7.5 cm) wide.

Having completed these basic preparations, it is now time to start experimenting with the consistencies and temperatures of the size and the oil colours. Test each colour individually (see chart) before attempting to use two colours or more together.

EQUIPMENT

1 Shallow tray
2 Mediumweight paper
3 Pins
4 Medicine droppers
5 Knitting needle
6 Marbling combs (see page 50)
7 Oil colours
8 Mixing jar
9 Ox-gall
10 White (mineral) spirit
11 Wallpaper paste
12 Measuring spoons
13 Measuring jug

TEST CHART

CAUTION It is essential that you skim the surface of the size with the strips of paper between each trial so that you can see clearly how the oil colours are reacting and also to get into the habit of skimming the surface between patterns.

■ If the colour disperses too thinly, there is too much ox-gall and you will have to add more thinned colour.

■ If the colour does not spread, there is not enough ox-gall – add more, drop by drop. If this does not work, it is possible that the size is too thick and more water should be stirred in carefully.

■ If the colour sinks through the size, it usually means that the size is too thick and should therefore be thinned.

■ If the colour still sinks, the temperature of the size may not be right. If the size feels warmer than room temperature, then add cold water to it, and if it feels colder, add warm water.

BASIC METHOD

1 Having achieved all the right consistencies, it is time to make a pattern. Drop colour randomly from a brush, loaded with colour, tapped against the side of the tray. Repeat with more colours, if desired.

2 Using a stick or knitting needle, draw patterns in the size by dragging the implement through the oil colours. Take care to work only on the surface of the size and move the pattern-making implement gently and fairly slowly so that you disturb the bath as little as possible.

3 When the pattern looks satisfactory, take a piece of lightweight to mediumweight paper by the opposite corners and lay it onto the size carefully, with a rolling movement. Do this fairly slowly or else air bubbles will become trapped beneath the paper, forming unintended white spaces in the pattern.

4 Lift off the paper almost immediately by picking up two adjacent corners and peeling it off the surface of the size.

5 Let it drain on the side of the tray for a minute or so and then lay it on some newspaper to dry. If you wish, you can rinse the paper very gently to remove the excess size, but this can affect the colour and is not really necessary. It is also possible to hang the paper on a line to dry.

CAUTION!!

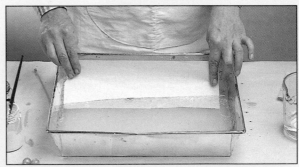

Remember to clean the excess colour from the surface of the size before you start to create the next pattern. Lay a sheet of clean paper onto the paste mixture to soak up any remaining colour.

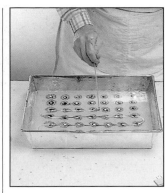

DESIGN VARIATIONS

1a Drop colour onto the size with a pipette (**far left**).

1b Repeat, dropping further colours onto the first colour (**middle left**).

1c With a knitting needle, draw through the centre of the dots to make a continuous thread (**left**).

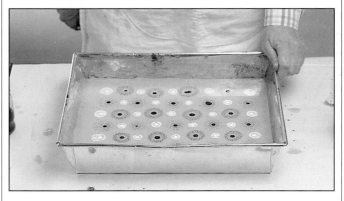

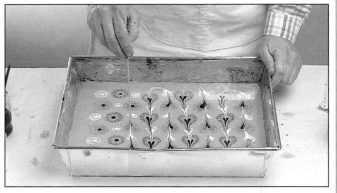

2a Alternatively, intersperse different- coloured drops of paint on the size.

2b Draw down through the rows of dots to feather the colours and create a design.

2c Agitate the surface slightly with the needle to make the lines of colour wavy.

2d Lay the paper slowly down onto the size.

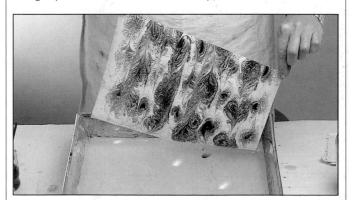

2e Quickly lift the paper off.

3a Alternatively, use larger movements to swirl the colours.

3b This produces a bolder, spiral design.

HOW TO MAKE A MARBLING COMB

1 Take 2 strips of card ½ in (1 cm) shorter than the width and/or length of the tray, and about 2 in (5 cm) wide. Mark off ½-in (1-cm) spaces on 1 strip.

2 Cover the edge of the strip with double-sided adhesive tape.

3 Position long pins on the tape at the marked points. Stick more tape to the other piece of card and stick the two cards together carefully.

4 Bang the 2 pieces firmly together with a hammer so that the cards are firmly stuck together. Additional combs can be made, setting different spaces for the 'teeth'.

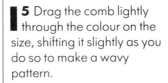

5 Drag the comb lightly through the colour on the size, shifting it slightly as you do so to make a wavy pattern.

Below Some decorative examples using these marbling techniques on coloured as well as white paper.

PAPIER MACHE

EQUIPMENT

■ Old newspapers
■ Coloured tissue paper
■ Wallpaper paste or thinned PVA adhesive
■ A mould
■ Petroleum jelly or plastic film
■ Scissors
■ Sandpaper
■ Paint brushes
■ Undercoat
■ Decorating materials and varnish

The craft (some would say art) of making objects out of papier mâché is almost as old as papermaking and was first practised by the Chinese. The objects they produced were practical and decorative, and were often made especially for festivals, when they were painted with religious images. In the 18th century, papier mâché had a resurgence of popularity in Europe and was used for many household pieces, from trays and boxes to tables and chairs, which were often highly decorated. Nowadays papier mâché is frequently used for theatre props, because it is simple to construct, lightweight, and, combined with modern epoxy glues, incredibly strong.

The term *papier mâché* is French and means 'chewed-up paper'. This describes the process very clearly: paper is torn into small pieces, glued and laid onto a mould. Several layers of paper are built up and, when the shape is thoroughly dry, it is removed from the mould, sanded smooth and decorated.

An alternative method is to make a papier mâché pulp or mash. It is complicated to prepare, but very easy to use. However, proprietary brands are now available for home use. In this book the basic 'strip and glue' method has been used.

BASIC METHOD

Prepare the working area by covering the table with newspaper. If you are using wallpaper paste, mix it according to the directions on the packet; if you are using PVA adhesive, dilute it with three parts glue to one part water.

Choose a mould with no under lip otherwise it will be impossible to remove the finished object. Now cover the mould with petroleum jelly or plastic film, so that the papier mâché object can be removed easily when the layers are dry.

TIPS

■ One way of keeping track of the completed layers is to use different types of paper for alternate layers – such as newspaper and coloured tissue paper. Eight layers is a good average for most articles.
■ Depending on the object, it may be wise to make the base thicker; for example, a wastepaper basket would benefit from the extra strength and weight of a thicker base.
■ The larger the article the longer it will take to dry.

1 Having torn up the newspaper and tissue, dampen the pieces, and lay neatly on the mould.

2 When the mould is covered, paint the surface liberally with the thinned adhesive or paste.

3 Now add the next layer.

4 When the mould is covered with this layer, brush on more adhesive. For a smooth result, try to work methodically so that the mould is covered evenly.

5 Put the mould in a warm place and leave it to dry for about 24 hours. Remove the shape from the mould carefully.

6 If necessary, trim the edges of the shape.

7 If the edge feels uneven or thin, it is possible to build up the shape at this stage.

8 Using medium- to fine-grade sandpaper, sand the article smooth and then paint it with two layers of undercoat. This ensures that the object has an even base on which to apply the final decoration.

Left There are many possibilities for decorating the finished object: you could apply collage or stencil a design onto it, see pages 34–7, or draw or paint onto it directly.

DECORATING PAPIER MACHE

BOWL 1 This bowl has such an open shape that the outside is barely visible.

Therefore, it is painted in a single colour and the inside is more decorative.

2 Cut a piece from a sheet of folded and dyed Japanese paper. Apply thinned PVA adhesive to the base of the bowl. Place the

cutout in position and press down gently as the dye may not be permanent and may spread.

3 Cut circles from coloured tissue paper and stick them round the edge of the bowl. Again take care when sticking these in position that the colour does not run.

4 When the first layer of circles is tacky, position the smaller circles and paint over them with another layer of PVA adhesive, which acts as a varnish. It is possible to use many overlapping layers of coloured tissue and work on a coloured background, which will affect the colours of the tissue. Try out various designs, using coloured paper for experiments.

Left The finished bowl, complete with decoration, makes an attractive container.

PLANT POT HOLDER

1 The plant pot holder here has been decorated with leaf stencils. These are made from lightweight paper so that they can be curved around the shape easily and attached to the holder with small pieces of plastic putty.

2 The holder was then sprayed with another layer of paint, in a well-ventilated space. You could achieve the same effect by painting onto the object with a brush.

Left The stencils were then removed. The inside was left undecorated because it will be hidden by the plant. Varnish was applied to the pot holder to make it waterproof.

▌WASTEPAPER RECEPTACLE

1 The outside was decorated with a collage of torn paper strips of newspaper and thin black paper.

▌**2** The strips were pasted and then positioned randomly around the shape.

▌**3** After positioning, the strips were trimmed to fit. They were allowed to overlap at the bottom, but were cut flush at the top.

▌**Left** The inside should be varnished or covered with enamel paint. The end result is original and effective, and simply achieved.

ORGAMI

Origami is a Japanese word which comes from the words *ori* (to fold) and *kami* or *gami* (paper). It was in Japan that the art first originated, some 1400 years ago. In its purest form, origami can be defined as the art of manipulating a paper square without the paper being cut, pasted, decorated or mutilated in any way; it may only be folded. This restrictive rule makes origami the most refined of all paper arts, but therein lies its beauty and wide appeal.

Only a few dozen traditional Japanese designs have come down to us, such as the flapping bird, crane, jumping frog or waterbomb (balloon). During the 1930s, though, the founding genius of modern origami – Akira Yoshizawa – came to realize that the art had enormous creative potential. Following his example, many other people around the world have created tens of thousands of new designs, some elegantly simple, others enormously complex. The designs range from animals to manmade objects and from expressive abstract forms to geometric solids.

Origami enthusiasts are particularly keen to form organized clubs. There are active groups all over the world and there is sure to be at least one in your own country. They cater for not just the expert but the complete novice too. Look for a club near to you in your telephone directory.

The designs that follow were originated by Paul Jackson, with the exception of the Printer's Hat and Japanese Box, both of which are traditional.

PAPER

Specialist Japanese shops often sell packets of squared, thin origami paper, brightly coloured on one side and white on the reverse. These papers are convenient to use, but can sometimes be expensive. Artists' supply stores and good stationers occasionally sell locally manufactured origami paper at a better price, though quality cannot be guaranteed.

If you are unable to buy special origami paper, any paper which can take a crease without cracking or unfolding is suitable. Good papers for practising on include typing paper, writing paper, brown wrapping paper, photocopy paper or computer paper. For making origami displays the best papers include gift-wrap papers (useful because they have a pattern or colour on one side and are white on the other), coloured photocopy paper and any attractive papers and paper-backed metallic foils found in artists' supply stores or stationers. Even thicker water-absorbent papers such as Ingres (or Strathmore) paper or watercolour paper are suitable if lightly dampened before folding. Unsuitable papers are newspaper, paper towels, tissues and clay-coated papers such as poster paper, as the coloured pigment cracks when folded.

If you cannot find papers with a different colour on either side, lay two differently coloured sheets back to back and fold them as one layer. Do not glue them together.

SYMBOLS

These symbols are the ABC of origami and will enable you to make the models which follow. Until you become familiar with them, keep referring back to this page. In particular, look at the different types of arrow.

mountain fold

existing crease

valley fold

(Fig 1)
Simple folds and creases

(Fig 2)
Fold to the front, or to the side

(Fig 3)
Fold behind

(Fig 4)
Fold, placing one spot on the other

(Fig 5)
X-ray view

(Fig 6)
Unfold crease(s)

(Fig 7)
Fold under or inside

(Fig 8)
Equal distances

TIPS ON FOLDING

■ Where possible, always fold against a hard, smooth surface such as a table or hard-backed book. Folding in the air is recommended for experts, but is difficult for beginners.

■ Follow the instructions carefully, looking closely at the drawings and reading the captions. Take particular note of the lettered corners.

■ Remember that the folds you are asked to make in one drawing will give you a shape which looks like the next drawing, so keep looking ahead to see what you are trying to achieve.

■ Fold slowly and neatly. Some models will take a little practice, so be ready to make them a few times before they look good.

PRINTER'S HAT

1 Begin with a double-page sheet from a broadsheet (large format) newspaper. Fold it in half from top to bottom. Then take the left edge to the right. Crease and unfold. Fold the top corners down to the centre crease.

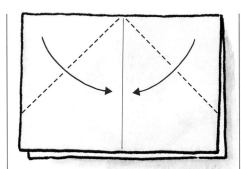

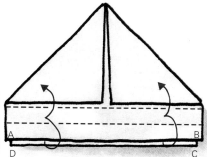

2 Fold the top layer edge AB up to the base of the triangles, then fold it up again along the base of the triangles . . .

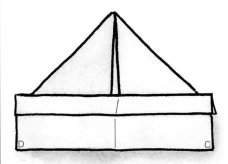

3 . . . to look like this. Turn the shape over.

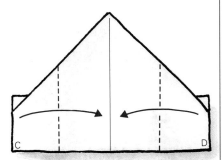

4 Fold the left and right edges C and D in to the centre crease.

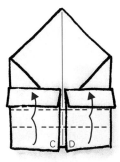

5 As in step 2, fold up the bottom edge CD to the base of the folds, and then fold them up again along the base of the folds.

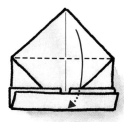

6 Fold down the top corner, tucking it underneath all the layers at the bottom.

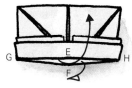

7 Separate E from F . . .

9 . . . in the middle. Flatten the shape into a square and crease the edges. Fold the right and left corners into the middle and tuck under the layers at G and H (**left**).

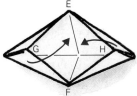

8 . . . pulling them further and further apart so that G and H come together . . .

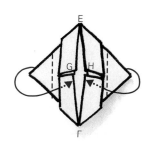

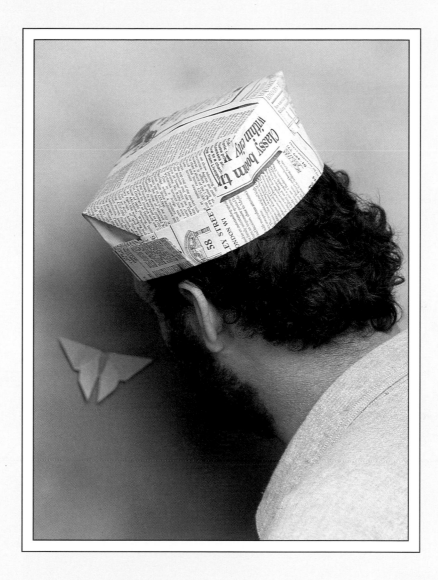

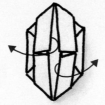 **10** Open up the shape and square off the sides.

 **11** The complete Printer's Hat.

BUTTERFLY

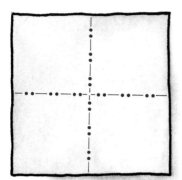

1 Make horizontal and vertical mountain creases.

2 Make diagonal valley folds.

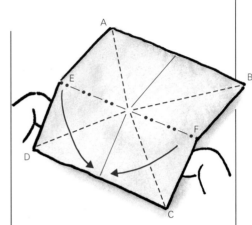

3 With DC on the table and AB up in the air, place your fingers behind E and F and pull them up and inwards . . .

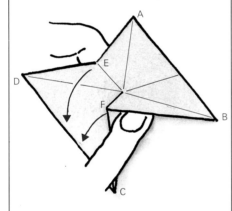

4 . . . like this, so that they lie together in the middle of edge DC . . .

5 . . . like this. Note how A lies on D and B on C.

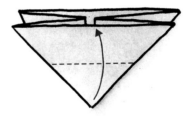

6 Turn the triangle upside down and fold the bottom corner up to the top edge.

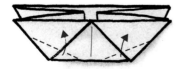

7 Fold in the bottom corners as shown.

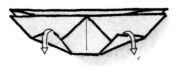

8 Unfold the corners.

9 Fold the bottom corners in again, but this time crease only the inner layers. Much of the crease is hidden inside the outer layer. Look at step 10.

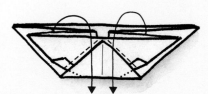

10 Pull down the top layer triangles.

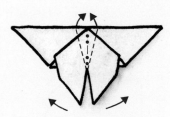

11 Make a central mountain crease, then two valley creases in the shape of a V, one on either side of the mountain. This pinches the centre of the butterfly to create a raised body and separates the lower wings.

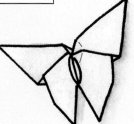

12 The complete butterfly.

CHATTERBOX

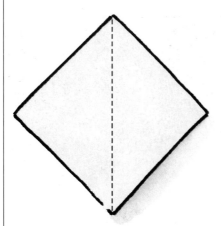

1 Make a valley fold along a vertical diagonal, and unfold.

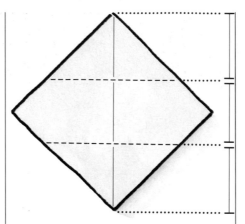

2 Carefully fold horizontal valley folds, which cross the diagonal crease at accurate thirds. Use a ruler to help you locate the creases. Unfold.

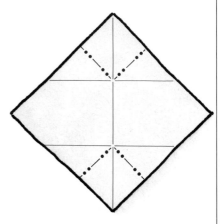

3 Make short mountain folds from the edges to the intersection of the steps 1 and 2 folds.

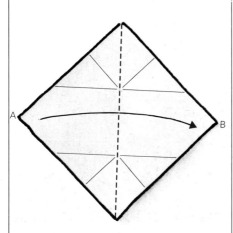

4 Fold the lefthand corner across to the right.

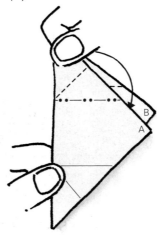

5 Grip the paper as shown. Push the top corner down in between layers A and B . . .

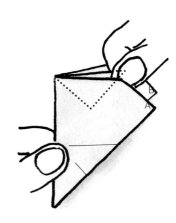

6 . . . like this. Flatten the paper.

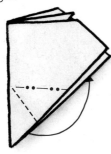

7 Repeat at the bottom.

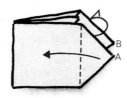

8 Fold A forwards to the left, and take B behind to the left.

9 Take the upper right edge and fold it forwards to the left edge; take the second right edge and fold it behind to the left edge, leaving the central spikes in place.

10 Fold the loose triangles in to the middle, two on the front, two on the back.

11 Partly unfold step 10, allowing the triangles to stand upright.

12 Draw in the eyes. Hold flap X at the front and back, one flap in each hand . . .

13 . . . and chatter away!

REPEAT PATTERN

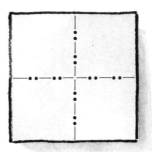

1 Make centre mountain creases, horizontally and vertically.

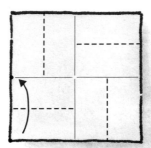

2 Fold the bottom edge of the paper up to the centre horizontal crease, but only press flat the left half of the paper, making a crease from the lefthand edge into the centre. Do this with all the other edges of the paper.

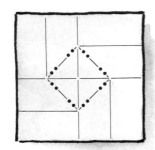

3 Make short diagonal mountain creases (or valley creases if you turn the paper over – this might be easier) connecting the points where steps 1 and 2 creases meet.

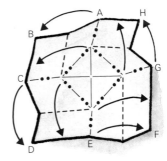

4 This step may be difficult, but persevere! Strengthen all creases. Simultaneously pinch the short mountain creases running into A, C, E and G and fold them over to corners B, D, F and H along the step 2 creases. This makes four pleats, contracts the paper and makes the centre diamond shape twist anticlockwise. All the creases move, twist and collapse together.

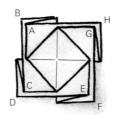

5 The flattened paper looks like this.

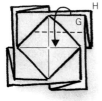

6 Bring the folded edge at the top of the paper (G) down to the centre.

7 Repeat with the three other folded edges.

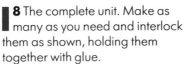

8 The complete unit. Make as many as you need and interlock them as shown, holding them together with glue.

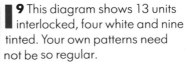

9 This diagram shows 13 units interlocked, four white and nine tinted. Your own patterns need not be so regular.

FISH NO 1

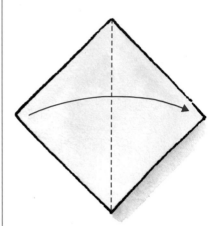

1 Valley fold the sheet in half along the vertical diagonal.

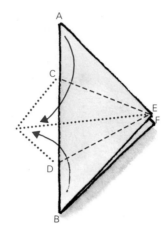

2 Fold corners A and B over to the left so that they touch. (Note that AC is longer than BD.)

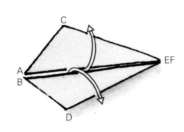

3 Unfold. (Note that triangle ACE is larger than BDE.)

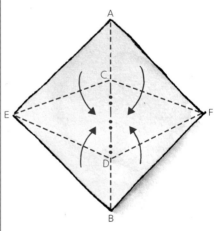

4 Refold all creases exactly as shown. Begin to fold along creases EC, CF, ED and DF, so that A and B come forward . . .

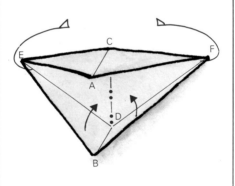

5 . . . like this. Bend E and F backwards so that they meet. A and B also meet . . .

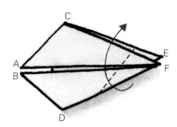

6 . . . like this. Fold up E and F as shown.

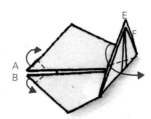

7 Pull down corner F to complete the tail. Turn corners A and B inside out, opening out each to do so.

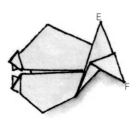

8 The complete fish . . .

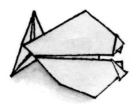

9 . . . and from the other side.

FISH NO 2

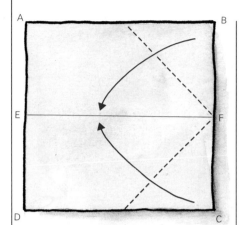

1 Fold a horizontal crease already made and unfold. Fold corners B and C in to the middle.

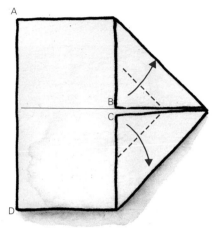

2 Fold B and C back out to the sloping edges.

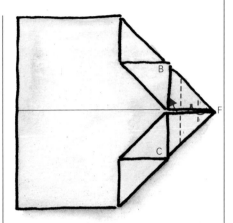

3 Fold corner F over twice to lie next to BC.

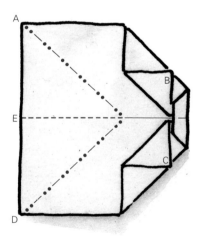

4 Carefully fold diagonal mountain folds, from corners A and D in to the middle and a horizontal valley fold from E to meet them. Begin to fold all three corners at once . . .

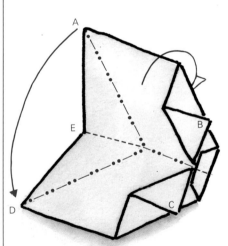

5 . . . so that the paper starts to collapse. A comes towards D. Note the mountain fold between B and C. Let A touch D.

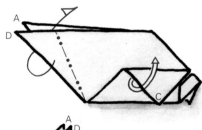
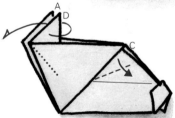

6 Fold D then A up through the centre. Unfold C (and B behind), (**top**). Twist D back out. Fold C forwards (and B behind), (**above**).

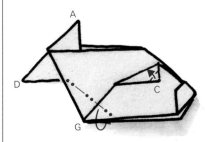

7 Fold back corner C to form an eye (and B behind). Push corner G under to the middle of the fish . . .

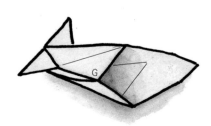

8 . . . to spread open the body, as seen here from underneath.

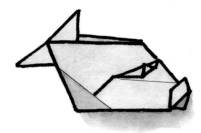

9 The complete fish.

HOW TO MAKE A MOBILE

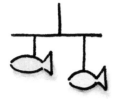

A mobile is a wonderful way of displaying what you make, particularly if it follows a theme, such as a shoal of fish. Placed in moving air near a window or door, the fish will spin slowly, each wire moving independently of the others to create constantly changing arrangements of fish.

Although spectacular, mobiles are surprisingly easy to construct. You do, however, need to follow a few basic rules.

The horizontal wires should be thin and lightweight. Wire rods from florists or model shops are ideal and can easily be cut to length with pliers or a hacksaw. Wooden rods such as dowel or canes are usable, but can look clumsy. Cotton or fine fishing line can be used to suspend the fish.

1 Attach lengths of thread to the balancing points of two origami fishes. Tie the other end of each thread to either end of a wire. Tie another thread tightly to the middle of that wire and slide it about until the wire is balanced exactly.

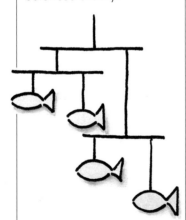

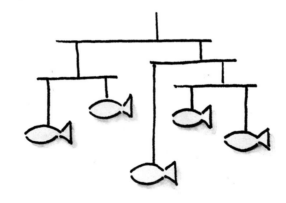

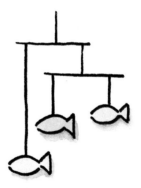

2 Repeat with another pair of fish. Attach each end of the loose threads to a wire, so that a pair of fish hang from each end. Attach a thread to the middle of the top wire and slide it about until the wire balances exactly.

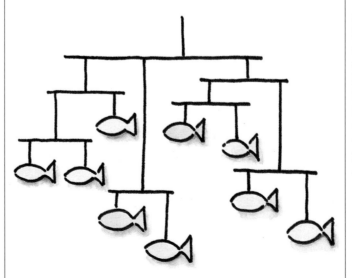

3 This process can be repeated as many times as you wish. Always design the mobile from the bottom up, making it balance at each level before progressing upward. Check that every fish can rotate through 360° without bumping into another.

JAPANESE BOX

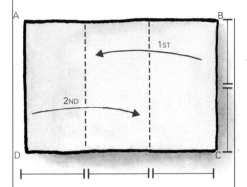

1 Begin with a 3 × 2 rectangle (one that measures three sections along one side to two sections along the adjacent side). Divide it into thirds, first folding BC across to the left, then fold AD across on top to the right.

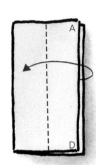

2 Fold AD back to the left edge.

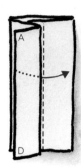

3 Pull out edge BC from under AD and fold it back to the right.

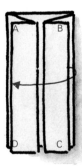

4 Unfold BC so that it meets and covers AD.

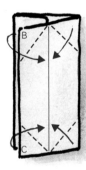

5 Turn in the four corners, the ones at B and C being single layers.

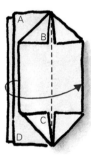

6 Fold BC back over to the right to meet the righthand edge.

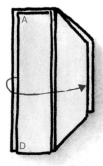

7 Unfold AD over to the right.

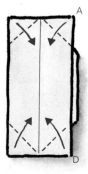

8 Turn in the four corners to meet the centre crease.

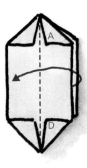

9 Fold AD back over to the left.

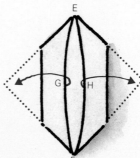

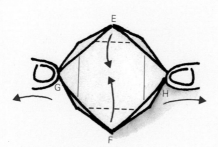

10 The paper is now symmetrical. Pull open the slit at G and H . . .

11 . . . opening up the box. Continue to pull so that as G and H separate, E and F come together in the middle . . .

12 . . . like this. Open up EF a little (**top**). The Japanese box is now complete, (**above**).

VALENTINE'S HEART

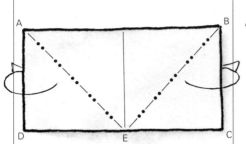

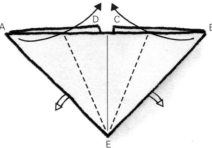

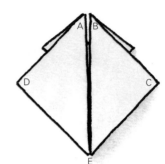

1 Begin with a 2 × 1 rectangle creased down the middle. Mountain fold corners C and D behind.

2 Fold edges AE and BE in to the centre crease, allowing D and C to swivel downwards and to the front . . .

3 . . . like this. Turn over.

4 Fold B and A downwards so that they lie at the folded edges running down to E.

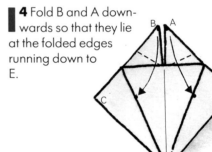

5 Tuck the loose corners into the pockets at B and A, locking B and A to the body of the paper. Fold in C and D as shown.

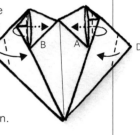

6 Turn over.

7 The complete Valentine's heart.

BOXES AND BAGS

EQUIPMENT

■ Sharp pencil and ruler
■ Knife and metal ruler
■ Cutting mat or scrap board
■ Scissors
■ Bone folder (if possible)
■ A pair of compasses
■ Protractor and/or set squares
■ Various glues
■ Various adhesive tapes
■ Thin card
■ Paper

This chapter opens up almost endless possibilities and many of the ideas are easily carried out. The most inexpensive gift can be made to look very special in its own box, and gifts which are awkward to wrap effectively can have their own custom-made box or bag.

The boxes should be made from thin card and the bags from various weights of paper, see pages 8–13. If coloured card (sometimes called board or art cover board) is not available, it is possible to glue gift-wrapping paper or decorated paper, see pages 32–50, to thin card. Make sure that the grain of both the card and the paper runs in the same direction, see page 9. Apply the glue evenly, but not excessively. Press the paper to remove any air bubbles.

When cutting curves you will achieve a smoother line if you keep the scissors in the same position while closing the blades slowly together and turning the card evenly with the other hand.

Score paper and card before you fold it because this helps to create a good crease. If possible, use a bone folder; otherwise, a blunt knife or the back of a scissors blade will do. If you are using a heavyweight card it may be necessary to cut through half the thickness of the card to achieve a good fold. Do this very carefully, using a craft knife or scalpel.

In order not to be wasteful, it may be wise for you to try out the more complicated boxes using paper first, before working on an expensive sheet of card. This is also a useful way of checking that the dimensions of the box are correct for the gift that you are planning to place within it.

In all the diagrams in this chapter the solid line should be cut and the dotted lines should be scored and a broken line represents a placement line. After you have removed the shape from its sheet and scored it, remember to fold all the lines to check the angles and the fit before you do any glueing. Small adjustments can often be made at this stage.

Glue flaps are used for all the projects in this chapter. They should be at least ½ in (1 cm) deep. If the shape is large, the glue flaps could be made up to 1 in (2.5 cm) deep. Tucking flaps are used on many of the boxes; these are always a little deeper than the glue flaps and can be cut at a more oblique angle to provide a tight fit.

Right These basic boxes were made from card which had been decorated using techniques described in the Decorating chapter, see pages 32–50.

BASIC BOX

When drawing a plan for a basic box, work out the dimensions and whatever the size, make sure that all angles are 90°, see Fig 1. The larger the box the thicker the card should be.

The number of flaps should equal the number of cut edges.

Use a sharp knife to cut out the shape, and cut away from the work – it would be infuriating to cut into the shape accidentally, having spent time carefully drawing it out.

Check the fit of the box, and stick the sides together, using a clear, all-purpose adhesive, rather than a glue stick. Next, stick the base in position. The box is now complete.

If you are using plain card you could decorate the outside, or cover the card with gift-wrapping paper. It is best to decorate or cover the card before assembling the box.

It is possible to make the basic box collapsible. Add the glue flaps to the base instead of the bottom of the sides, and then stick only the side glue flap in position. The box can now be flattened and assembled when required. But remember that the box will not be as strong as a rigid one and do not forget to stick the base in place so that the bottom does not fall out of the box at the wrong moment!

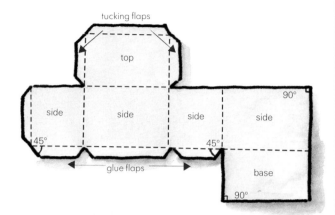

tucking flaps

top

side | side | side | side

90°

45°   45°

glue flaps

base

90°

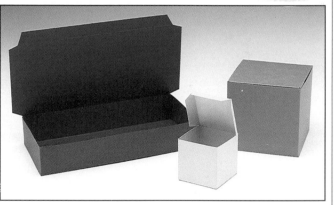

Above These three boxes were made from plain-coloured card with different dimensions using the basic method.

TWO-PIECE BOX

A two-piece box can be as simple as the silver box in the photograph, or more complicated, like the red one with the star shape. A two-piece box is more economical to make than the basic box, but cannot be collapsed.

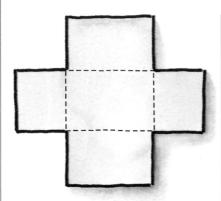

1a The easiest way to make a box with a separate lid is to cut out the box shape to the required size and to stick the sides together, using adhesive tape (decorated adhesive tape is very effective here).

1b Make the lid in exactly the same way, but make the sides very short; the dimensions of the rectangle should be 1/16 in (1.5 mm) larger in both directions to accommodate the thickness of the card.

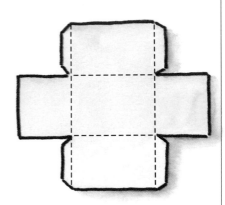

1c If adhesive tape is not suitable or available, the same result can be achieved by adding glue flaps. Make sure the allowance for the card thickness is generous when you are making the lid because the glue flaps will increase the thickness.

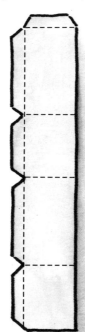

2a To make the blue box in the photograph, mark out a strip of card which is equal in length to twice the length and twice the width of the gift plus a glue flap, and equal to the height of the gift plus a glue flap. The strip can have joins if necessary. Cut out, score the folds and glue to form a box.

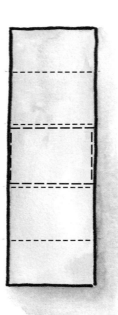

2b For the wrap-around lid, mark out a piece of card measuring the length of the gift by twice the width and twice the height plus an overlap. Cut out and score the folds.

2c Glue the centre section of the lid to the glue flaps at the base of the box. Fold the side and top pieces around the box, enclosing the gift. Either tie it to close or seal with a sticker.

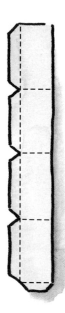

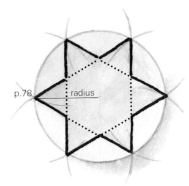

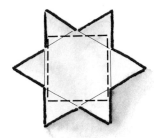

3a To make the red star-shaped box, mark out a strip of card (see 2a), but with the sides of equal measure to form a square box. Make the lid in the same way, but slightly larger.

3b To construct the star, measure the length of one side of the box with the compasses. This is the radius of the circle. Draw the circle. Keeping the same radius setting, place the point of the compasses on the circumference of the circle and mark the point it crosses on the curve. Move the compass to this point and repeat the process until you have six points around the circumference. Join alternate points with a pencil and ruler.

3c Cut out two star shapes and glue one to the flaps at the base of the box and the other to the flaps at the top of the lid. The box is now complete.

Below The possibilities for decorating homemade boxes are endless. Decorated adhesive tape, stickers and attractive ties all add a professional finishing touch. The basket-type box was made using metallic strips of card woven together, see pages 32–3, with a simple strip attached to act as a handle.

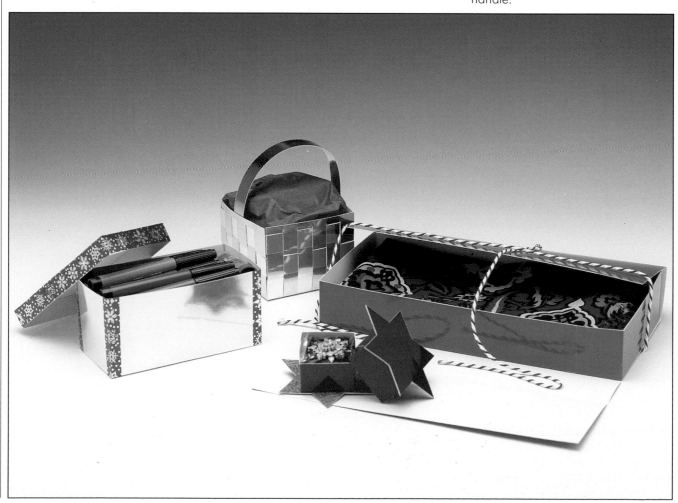

COVERING BOXES

Boxes can be re-used; chocolate and soap boxes particularly are often a suitable size for other gifts. There are two ways of disguising their previous uses. Often it is necessary only to re-cover the lid, but the method is the same if the bottom is also being re-covered.

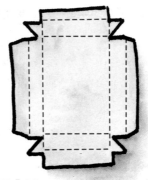

1 Measure the width and length of the box lid and the height of the box sides. The piece of paper will need to be big enough for the lid measurement plus four times the sides. Draw the rectangle in the centre of a piece of lightweight paper; add sides all around and then add another set of sides to turn in. Draw 'ears' as in the diagram.

2 Cut out, score and fold the whole shape. Position the box on the drawn rectangle, turn the 'ears' inwards.

3 Stick the 'ears' and the turn-in allowance down.

4 Then stick the opposite sides.

VARIATIONS

Many interesting patterns can be made using corrugated paper; the boxes in the photograph (**right**) show two designs. Always cut the corrugated paper with a sharp knife on the wrong (flat) side without pressing hard, because this would flatten the 'ribs'. Use a fairly strong adhesive. Cover the top first and then, with the covered top downwards, wrap a strip of the corrugated paper around the sides.

COMPLEX BOXES

Above Basic plan for the flat gift holder.

FLAT GIFT HOLDER

This type of box is most suitable for flat gifts, such as scarves and ties. Measure the gift and then make the gift holder the length of the gift, and the width plus the height of the gift (if the gift is solid, allow a little extra). At its deepest point, the curves at the top and bottom of the holder should measure approximately twice the height of the gift.

With these measurements it is now possible to draw the plan of the gift holder, see diagram. The curve can either be drawn with the compasses, placed on the centre line, or using a dinner plate of suitable size. Join two sides with one curve and trace this off onto a piece of scrap card and use this as a template to draw the other curves. Cut out and score. Stick the glue flap to the side. Place the gift in the holder and close by turning in the curves.

To make the gift holder extra-special, a shape, a butterfly for example, can be cut and folded from the right side; stick a piece of decorative paper underneath and lift the cut-out.

Below The blue gift holder is decorated with a butterfly-shape cut out (see main text). The green one was made with lightweight card that had been decorated with a stencilled design, see pages 35–7.

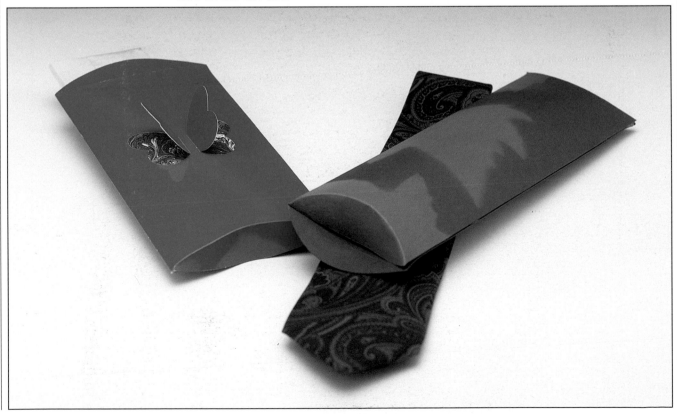

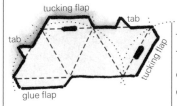

tucking flap

tab

tab

tucking flap

glue flap

■ **Above** Basic plan for the pyramid box.

PYRAMID BOX

This little box can either be used as a box or as a decoration. The size is variable. Start by drawing a line and draw a semicircle on this line. Place the compass point, with the same radius, at one end of the semicircle and mark the centre and the point it crosses on the curve. Repeat from the other end. With the same radius setting, draw another semicircle so that it joins the first. Put the compass point on the join and mark the point it crosses on this curve. Join all the marks, and four equilateral triangles will emerge. Add one glue flap to the base of the first triangle, two tucking flaps with slits, and two tabs to correspond with the slits, see diagram. Cut out the basic shape and score all the other lines. Stick the glue flap and place the gift inside and close the box tightly with the tabs — it is quite tricky to tuck in the tabs but ensures a very secure closure.

■ **Below** You can make your pyramid box to any size. Use plain or foiled light card, or decorate using the techniques described in the Decorating Chapter.

HEXAGONAL BOX

This box looks most impressive and is not as complicated as it appears. Once the size of the hexagon has been worked out it is quite easy to construct. If the box is being used for a circular gift this must fit *within* the hexagon and this should be worked out using scrap paper.

Draw a circle larger than the gift. Draw a horizontal line through the middle of the circle. Using the same radius setting, place the compass point on one of the intersections and mark the point it crosses on the curve. Move the compass to this point and repeat until you have six points around the circumference. Join these points and check whether the gift will fit into this hexagon – if not try again. Once this is correct, draw a plan following the diagram. The sides of the box are equal to the height of the gift and one side of the hexagon in length. The three flaps, top and bottom, are half the height of the hexagon. Cut out, score and fold. Check the angles of the flaps before glueing, in case any adjustments need to be made. Stick the glue flap and assemble the box. If necessary, stick down the tucking flaps on the base so that the box does not fall apart if the gift is heavy.

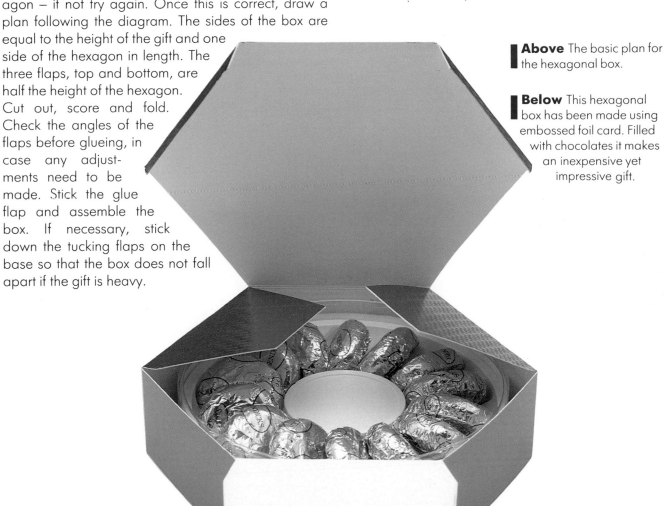

Above The basic plan for the hexagonal box.

Below This hexagonal box has been made using embossed foil card. Filled with chocolates it makes an inexpensive yet impressive gift.

PAPER SHOPPING BAGS

These bags are easy to make and can look extremely decorative. They can be made in many different sizes — tall and thin for bottles, short and wide for cosmetic items — and from many different types of paper. Matching gift tags, see page 92, can be added. Unusual handles can be made from toning or contrasting materials, such as plaited wool or ribbons.

Once you have mastered the basic method many variations are possible. Bags can be made in any size using normal gift-wrapping, but the larger the bag the thicker the paper will need to be. It is also possible to use plain paper and decorate it before assembly, see pages 32–50.

There are a few basic rules: all angles should be right angles (90°) so that the bag stands square when finished; the bottom flaps should be about ½ in (1 cm) less than the width of the sides; score the fold lines to give a crisper crease; this is essential on thicker paper and card.

BASIC BAG

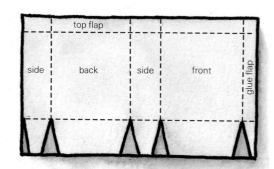

1 It is easiest to work on the wrong side of the paper. Decide on the size of the bag and draw the plan. Cut out the shape, removing the shaded areas. Score the dotted lines lightly, and fold and then unfold them.

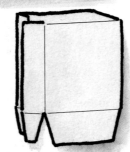

2 Glue down the top flap, which adds strength and looks neater. Next glue the front flap to the side.

3 Finally, glue the bottom flaps to each other — the side flaps to the back flap and the front flap on top of the side flaps.

Left For the handles, punch holes in the top edge and thread ribbons, cord or braid through them. The holes can act as closures or can be simply decorative.

STRONG PAPER BAG

Making a bag which will carry a bottle or a heavy or large gift poses a few problems, but these can easily be overcome.

If a bottle or heavy gift is to be placed in the bag, it is advisable to glue a piece of card inside the base of the bag. To strengthen the top of the bag, add an extra strip of paper under the top flap. The basic plan is the same as for the ordinary bag, page 84, except that the measurements for all the sides will be identical and should be the diameter of the bottle plus ¼ in (6 mm). The height of the bag should be 2½ in (6 cm) more than the height of the bottle, so that the top edges can be drawn together.

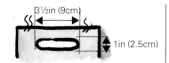

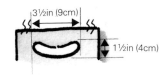

■ When making a large bag it is quite simple to add a strong handle. Cut a piece of plain lightweight card the width of the bag and at least 3 in (7.5 cm) deep. Cut the hand shape out of the centre of the card and mark this hole on the bag plan. Cut these holes out of the paper on the bag and top flap, and glue the card stiffener in position. Continue as for the basic bag.

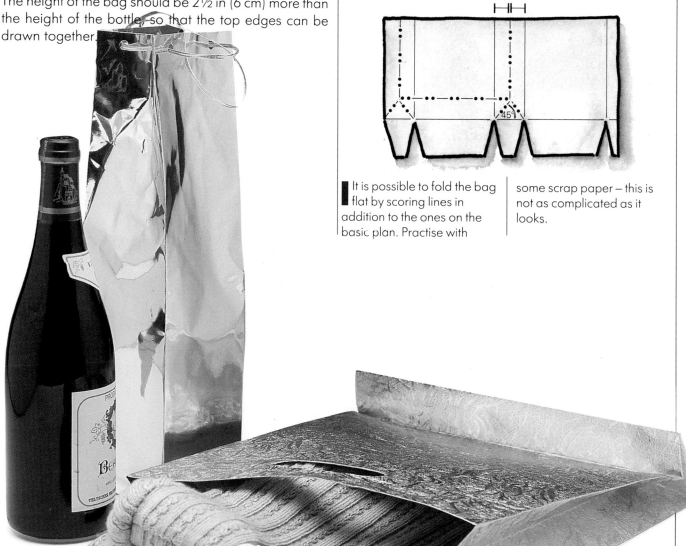

■ It is possible to fold the bag flat by scoring lines in addition to the ones on the basic plan. Practise with some scrap paper – this is not as complicated as it looks.

HEART-SHAPED BAG

The decorative heart-shaped bag shown on this page is deceptively simple. The design is based on a semi-circle and can be made from many different types of paper or card. It is easy to alter the size by following the directions.

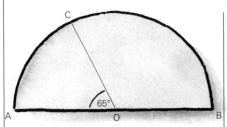

1 Draw a semicircle and mark a point about 65° from one edge, at C.

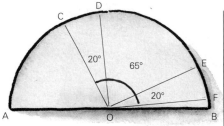

2 Mark another point 20° from C, then another at 65° and another at 20°. Join all these points to the centre.

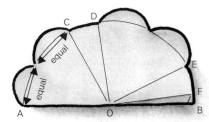

3 Now divide both of the largest arcs in half, either by measuring or using a protractor. Draw semicircles on each half.

Below Punch holes in the side panels and make handles. Decorate the bag if you wish. For inspiration see pages 32–50.

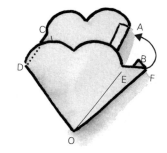

4 Cut out the whole shape and score all lines from the centre out to the edge and fold. Glue the shaded area to the heart shape.

WRAPPING IDEAS

The art of wrapping and the art of giving could be said to be one and the same. A beautifully wrapped box shows that you have chosen and wrapped a gift with care.

The ideas in this chapter offer a basic introduction to the art of wrapping. The secret is to choose your wrapping papers with care, then to fold them neatly. Accessories such as ribbons, bows or gift tags are important decorative features which help to personalize a gift, but they will not disguise a badly wrapped box.

Almost any paper can be used to wrap a gift. Con-ventional, patterned, gift-wrap papers are good, but consider using more unusual papers such as tissue paper, Ingres (Strathmore) paper and other papers from artists' supply stores and stationers. In particular, consider using decorated papers, see pages 32–50. A hand-decorated wrapping paper will give your gift a special personal touch that will have great meaning for the receiver. Some decorating techniques, such as folding and dipping, see pages 42–5, are best done with paper that is too thin to use as wrapping, so back them with another sheet for extra strength.

THE PERFECT WRAP

This is the best way to wrap a box so that it looks neat and well folded. The method will work for a box of any shape.

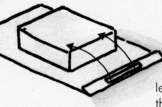

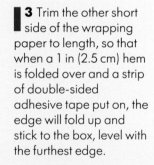

3 Trim the other short side of the wrapping paper to length, so that when a 1 in (2.5 cm) hem is folded over and a strip of double-sided adhesive tape put on, the edge will fold up and stick to the box, level with the furthest edge.

1 Place the gift box on the wrapping paper. Trim the long edges of the sheet so that the overlap at the sides is the same as the height of the box. Fold over a hem of 1 in (2.5 cm) along one short edge.

2 Fix a strip of double-sided adhesive tape to the hem, almost the length of the box. Peel off the backing then stick the hem to the top of the box 2 in (5 cm) beyond the nearside edge.

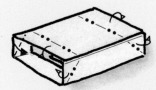

4 Push in the sheet as shown. Be careful to keep it neat.

5 Fold in side triangles to lie flat against the box, forming a tapered point at the bottom.

6 Fix a small piece of double-sided adhesive tape to the tapered point at the bottom and fold up.

7 The box complete. Reinforce all the creases as the finishing touch.

PLEATED WRAPS

Here are three simple ways to pleat a sheet of wrapping paper to hold a name tag, a sheet of complementary wrapping paper or a decorative form. As ever, be careful to fold as neatly as possible, perhaps practising on scrap paper first.

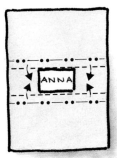

1a For each, first make your item to be inserted between the pleats, preferably from thick paper or card. It can be any size, but the larger it is the farther apart the pleats will be. Place the card in the middle of the wrapping paper.

1b Carefully construct two pleats across the top and bottom of the inserted card so that the top pleat folds downwards and the bottom one folds upwards, trapping it between the pleats. The depth of the pleats should be at least ¾ in (2 cm).

1c Continue to wrap as described in 'The Perfect Wrap' above. This will create a wrapped gift with pleats running down the length of the box.

TIPS

Try experimenting with other patterns of pleats to create practical or decorative features on a gift-wrapped box: horizontal pleats crossing vertical pleats; pleats across a corner; lines of parallel pleats and so on. The effects can be surprisingly creative.

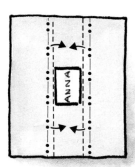

2a Here the pleats run along the length of the wrap, so that in the finished wrap they lie across the box.

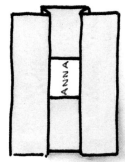

2b Construct the pleats and fold over the card as before.

2c Complete the wrap.

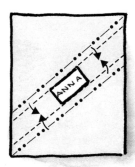

3a An unusual variation. Lay the card at an angle in the middle of the wrapping paper and form the pleats as before.

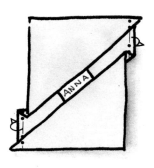

3b Fold the excess paper behind (or cut it off), to restore the rectangular shape of the sheet.

3c Wrap as before to create a band of pleats set at an angle to the sides of the box.

RIBBONS AND BOWS

RIBBONS

Ribbons are excellent ways to turn a plainly wrapped box into an attractively wrapped gift. Not all gift boxes need ribbons though – those that are wrapped in elaborately patterned gift-wrap paper may well be attractive enough as they are, or perhaps with an additional bow or gift tag.

Long lengths of gift-wrap ribbon can be purchased in many gift shops or stationers. Exciting and unconventional ribbons can be found in the fabric departments of stores. These range from hair ribbons to lace edging. Homemade ribbons can be made using strips cut from large sheets of paper decorated using the techniques described on pages 32–50. Alternatively, plaited wools make pretty ribbons.

An interesting use of ribbon is to plait or weave together two or more colours. The 'under-and-over' pattern can vary and the ribbons can either be set square onto the box or set at an angle. See below for further ideas. Be careful not to cover too much of the gift with ribbons, or it may look over-decorated.

BOWS

Intricate bows already made up can often be purchased from gift shops or stationers, particularly in the weeks before Christmas. They are awkward to make well at home, requiring the construction of wooden templates and a lot of practice.

Here, though, is a simple but very attractive bow, sometimes called 'My Lady'. It works equally well made from gift-wrap ribbon, fabric ribbon or paper strips.

1 Cut a length of ribbon about 22 in (56 cm) long and twist it as shown, being careful to make both loops the same size. Secure the centre with a staple .

2 Cut another length of ribbon about 13 in (33 cm) long and form three loops as shown, beginning with the middle one. Trim off any excess. Check that it will fit between the loops of the other piece of ribbon.

3 Staple the second piece of ribbon to the first, being careful to line up all the layers and to centralize the second piece on top. To complete the bow, cut a V-shaped notch into the ends of the ribbon.

GIFT TAGS

Gift tags are one of the finishing touches of a present and a little imagination can make even this small piece of paper quite special. They can be quick and easy to make or quite intricate.

Gift tags can be single or double. They can be attached with a punched hole and cord or stuck directly onto the parcel. There are many types of cord available in the shops with which to attach the tag – plait together threads that tone with the colours from the paper design; ribbons; wool or metallic string.

Use card cut to the required size or shape, scored and folded, if making a double card. If you use paper, it may be necessary to glue this to another piece of paper so that it is not too floppy. This method could also be used to make a card from the paper used to wrap the gift.

Plain tags can be decorated with stickers, quilled shapes (see below) and miniature origami.

QUILLS

- Strips of paper
- Glue
- Cocktail sticks, matchsticks or dowel rod
- Scissors – optional
- Tweezers – optional
- Waxed paper

Quilling uses rolled strips of paper to form shapes, which can be glued together to make patterns. The designs can then be used in numerous ways, for example, glued on cards for gift tags or greetings cards, as decorations for boxes, as mobiles or stencils. Quilling is sometimes known as paper filigree and was used by monks in the 15th century to make panels of imitation gold filigree. In the Victorian period quilling was considered a very lady-like pursuit and tea-caddies were a popular item for decoration.

Traditionally the strips are ⅛ in (3 mm) wide and the length can vary. The strips can sometimes be bought in stationery shops or can be laboriously cut by hand, or carnival streamers can be used – these are usually a little wider, but the principle remains the same.

Using a cocktail stick, matchstick or thin dowel rod with a split, place one end of the strip in the split and turn it slowly and evenly so that the strip remains level. When the paper is completely rolled, squeeze it lightly to make a tight curve before removing the stick. This coil is a loose open coil.

BASIC COILS

- Loose open coil.

- Loose coil with the end stuck down. Most shapes are made from the loose coil.

- Tight coil – the end is glued before removing from the stick.

- Pear drop – squeeze the side that has been stuck, to a point.

- Petal – as pear drop but curved gently at the same time as squeezing to form the point.

- Eye-shape – both ends are pointed and the whole shape is elongated slightly.

- Leaf-shape – as eye-shape but curved gently in both directions.

DECORATING WITH QUILLS

Patterns can be planned in advance or built up as you go along. In either case, it is best to work on a piece of waxed paper so that the design can be moved around as the work progresses, without getting stuck. This is especially important if the piece is to be used on its own. If the design is being made as a decoration for an object, it can be worked directly onto the object by glueing the centre of the shape and placing each part carefully in position. Tweezers or an extra cocktail stick will be useful. Finished designs can be sprayed with paint or varnish.

■ V-shape – creased at the halfway point and rolled outwards.

■ Heart-shape – as V-shape but rolled inwards.

■ Triangle – squeezed in three places.

■ S-shape – rolled in opposite directions from both ends.

■ Scroll-shape – rolled in the same direction from both ends.

TWIST-OUTS, CUT-AWAYS AND POP-UPS

These three similar techniques are exciting ways to create imaginative three-dimensional greetings cards or decorations. They are all simple to make, but will be best understood if you first follow the instructions that explain how to produce a basic example of each technique.

TWIST-OUTS

Twist-outs are particularly ingenious ways to create three-dimensional cards, suspended decorations or simply beautiful shapes to be admired. Use thin card for finished examples — paper is too weak and thick card too cumbersome to bend easily.

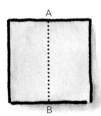

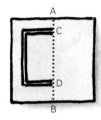

1 For the basic method, draw line AB down the centre of a piece of scrap card or paper.

2 With a blade, incise line C to D, so that the incision starts and ends on AB. (Note that AC is shorter than DB.)

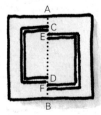

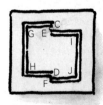

3 Next, incise line E to F, so that the incision once again starts and ends on AB. Note that E is below C and F is below D.

4 Pull edge GH towards you and push IJ away from you, forming short creases between CE and DF.

5 The centre of the card will twist out from its frame.

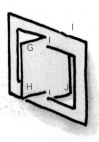

Below right This technique, once mastered, will produce decorations and sculptural forms of great beauty. Study the examples in the photograph, then experiment with your own ideas.

VARIATIONS

The following are variations of the basic technique. The principle is that line AB can be anywhere on a sheet of card. The incisions can be any shape, but they must begin and end on AB, so that CE and DF can be creased along one uninterrupted line.

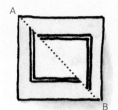

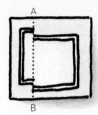

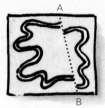

▌Draw AB along a diagonal, so that when incisions are made, the centre twists out from its frame along a diagonal axis.

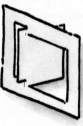

▌Draw AB towards the lefthand edge, so that the centre twists out a long way on the right but very little on the left.

▌Draw AB in an arbitrary position and doodle incisions on it at random.

GREETINGS CARDS

Here are three twist-outs in the form of greetings cards.
The letters could be re-worked to say HAPPY BIRTH-
DAY, GET WELL, GOOD LUCK, etc.

Other good festive themes include candles, stars,
baubles or stockings.

■ If you draw AB on the
horizontal, this creates
possibilities for sculptural
cards on a wide variety of
themes, including all
those suggested above.
Remember, any shape —
no matter how unlikely —
can be made to twist out.
Invent your own to suit an
occasion which requires
you to send a card.

Below left Twist-outs make highly individual greetings cards. The wordings and figurations can be altered to suit every occasion.

Below right Concentric twist-outs make fascinating mobiles. Simply thread a strong piece of thread through the middle of the outer frame.

CONCENTRIC DESIGNS

Once you have understood and practised the basic twist-out technique, try making concentric incisions.

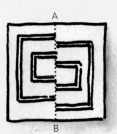

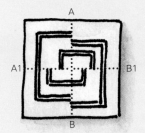

The simplest way of doing this is to retain AB as the single line along which all incisions start and end. Cut all the incisions, then twist out each alternate frame, working towards the centre.

An intriguing elaboration is to introduce a second line (A_1B_1) on which to start and end incisions. Whereas the previous design creates vertical frames, this will also produce horizontal ones. Other lines (A_2B_2, A_3B_3 etc.) may be introduced to make concentric shapes twist out at many different angles.

CUT-AWAYS

This easy technique is an interesting way to make a shape of card project beyond a crease, creating an unusual silhouette. It looks particularly good when used on a greetings card. Use card of thin to medium thickness.

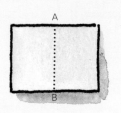

BASIC METHOD

1 Draw line AB down the middle.

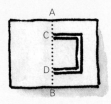

2 With a blade, incise line C to D starting and ending on AB.

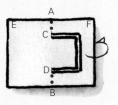

3 Make a mountain crease between AC and DB, so that corner F bends backwards to touch E. Do not crease between C and D.

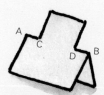

4 The card should look like this, with a rectangle of card projecting beyond the crease.

VARIATIONS

| You could make a cut-away nose and pipe, with the outline of the other half of the card cut to the profile of a head.

| Here the card beyond the heart has been lost to one side of crease AB.

| When the top half of the numerals are made to project

beyond the crease, the card beyond the bottom half of the numerals can be cut away to complete their silhouettes.

POP-UPS

Of the three techniques explained in this chapter, pop-ups can become the most technical. This section shows how versatile the simpler pop-up techniques are. If you wish to see more complex examples, look at some of the remarkably clever pop-up books in the children's section of a good bookshop. Pop-ups can be used in combination with the cut-away techniques explained in the previous section, helping to break the symmetry of a pop-up shape. Use thin card, but practise on stiff paper.

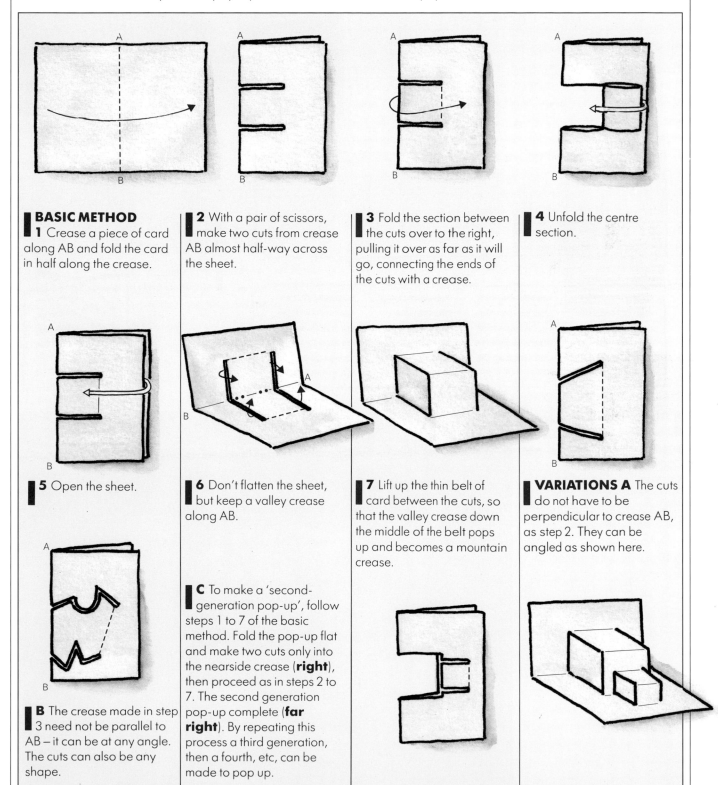

BASIC METHOD
1 Crease a piece of card along AB and fold the card in half along the crease.

2 With a pair of scissors, make two cuts from crease AB almost half-way across the sheet.

3 Fold the section between the cuts over to the right, pulling it over as far as it will go, connecting the ends of the cuts with a crease.

4 Unfold the centre section.

5 Open the sheet.

6 Don't flatten the sheet, but keep a valley crease along AB.

7 Lift up the thin belt of card between the cuts, so that the valley crease down the middle of the belt pops up and becomes a mountain crease.

VARIATIONS A The cuts do not have to be perpendicular to crease AB, as step 2. They can be angled as shown here.

B The crease made in step 3 need not be parallel to AB – it can be at any angle. The cuts can also be any shape.

C To make a 'second-generation pop-up', follow steps 1 to 7 of the basic method. Fold the pop-up flat and make two cuts only into the nearside crease (**right**), then proceed as in steps 2 to 7. The second generation pop-up complete (**far right**). By repeating this process a third generation, then a fourth, etc, can be made to pop up.

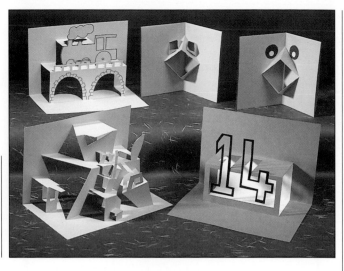

MULTI POP-UPS

The pop-ups made so far have all been built up from a central crease AB (see step 1). However, by starting with more than one crease, you can make decorations which are fully three-dimensional. Here is one suggestion.

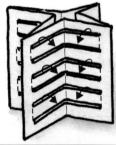

1 Cut out a piece of thin card four times as long as it is high, with a small tab on the end for glueing. Pleat it into eighths, alternating the mountain and valley creases.

2 Make 24 cuts as shown.

3 Pleat the strip and glue the tab to hold the pleats in the shape of a cross. Pull out the belts of card between the cuts.

Above right
Suggestions for pop-up cards are illustrated here. Some are first-generation pop-ups, some have two or more generations, and others have incorporated cut-away techniques.

Right The cross-shape opened out, with suggested variations.

STATIONERY

CARD FOLDS AND IDEAS

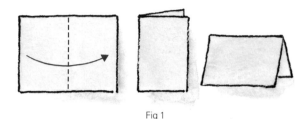

Fig 1

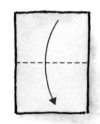

Fig 2

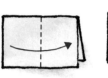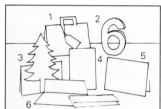

Left These cards are all made from the basic folds shown above: 1 and 2 are designs cut from a single fold (see Fig 1); 3 is a single fold with a cut-out shape glued on; 4 is a double fold (see Fig 2) with a paper weaving decoration attached to the face; 5 is a single fold decorated with a collage made of adhesive-backed paper; 6 is a single fold card with a basic envelope, see page 106.

CARD FOLDS AND IDEAS

There are many ways to fold a piece of card or paper to form the basis of a greetings card. Some are simple and well known, whereas others are a little more complicated. The illustrations here show some basic starting points and the photographs indicate how they can be made into attractive greetings cards. Use thin card, except for Figs 2, 6 and 7, for which thicker paper is best. See page 8 for a guide to paper and card weights.

The techniques shown in other chapters of the book can be adapted to form cards, especially those in Decorating Paper (pages 32–50), Origami (pages 58–74) and Twist-outs, Cut-aways and Pop-ups (pages 96–102). Think of the type of card fold and paper technique that best suit the occasion – the variations are endless.

ADDITIONAL FOLDS

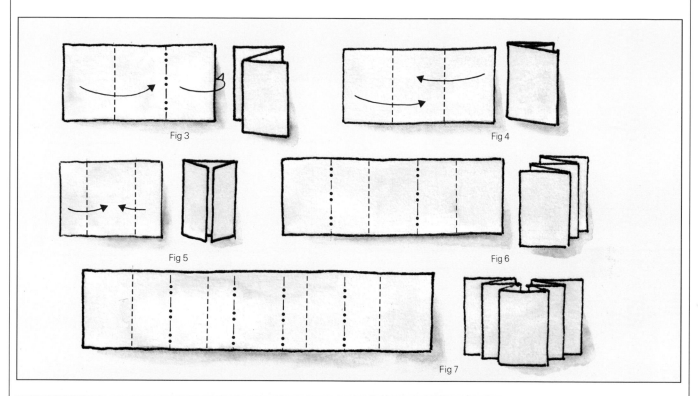

Fig 3

Fig 4

Fig 5

Fig 6

Fig 7

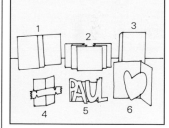

Left Most of these cards are made from folds shown above: 1 is made from the fold in Fig 6; 2 is made from the fold shown in Fig 7 and decorated with purchased stickers; 3 is made from the fold in Fig 4 – the righthand flap has been cut out to act as a mount for the photograph; 4 and 5 are made from the fold in Fig 5 and are both cut-outs; 6 is made from the fold in Fig 2 using the pop-up technique explained on page 101.

BASIC ENVELOPE

Having practised some of the techniques in the previous chapters, it will no longer be necessary for you to buy greetings cards or even an envelope to fit any card, because you will be able to make your own. It is also easy to decorate stationery and to make a holder as a really unusual gift.

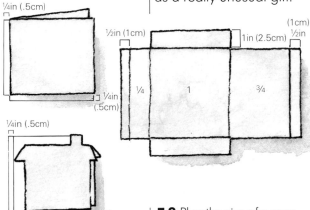

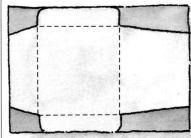

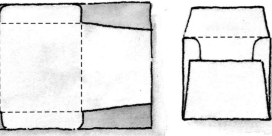

1 Measure the card and add ¼ in (½ cm) to the length and the width (**top**). If the card is an irregular shape (**above**) add extra to the widest points.

2 Plan the size of paper required for the envelope: the side flaps should be at least 1 in (2.5 cm); the bottom flap should be three-quarters the width of the card plus ½ in (1 cm) for closing; and the top flap should be a quarter the width plus ½ in (1 cm).

3 Draw this shape on your chosen paper and cut it out. (Use a coin to draw the curves of the slide flaps.) Taper the top and bottom flaps. Score the dotted lines.

4 Turn in the side flaps. Apply glue to the side edges of the bottom flap, turn it up and stick it to the side flaps. The envelope is now ready to be used. To close the envelope, either use glue or double-sided adhesive tape along the top flap.

Left You could line the basic envelope using plain coloured tissue paper or folded and dyed paper, see pages 42–5. Add the lining before you turn in the side flaps. Cut a piece of lining paper the width of the envelope and the length of the envelope minus the bottom flap. Glue it in position before assembling the envelope.

Right The envelopes in the photograph have been folded from a piece of paper the same size as the pieces on which they are lying.

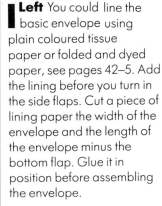

FOLDED ENVELOPE 1

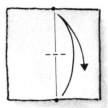

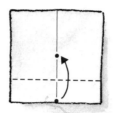

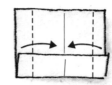

1 Begin with a square of paper, creased vertically down the middle. Fold the bottom edge up to the top and press it flat in the middle to find the mid-point of the square.

2 Fold the bottom edge up to the centre.

3 Fold in the sides, as shown.

4 Fold the loose corners behind at the bottom.

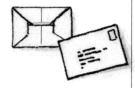

5 Fold the top corners into the centre vertical crease.

6 Crease across the base of the top triangles, tucking them inside the pocket. This locks the envelope shut.

7 The complete envelope. Write the address on the side without any folds.

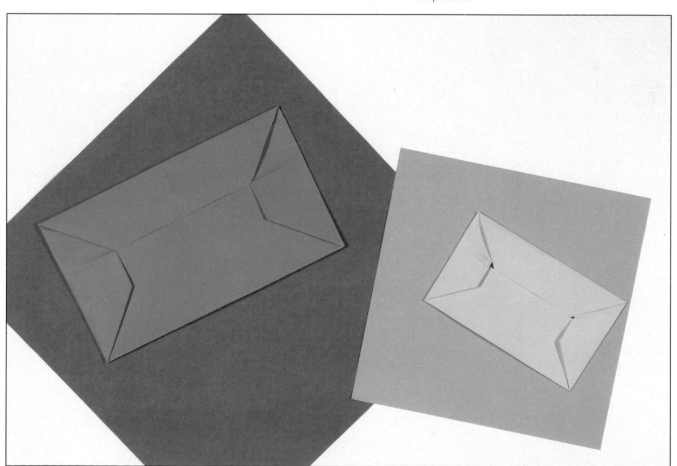

FOLDED ENVELOPE 2

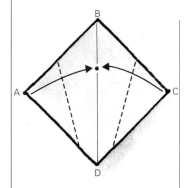

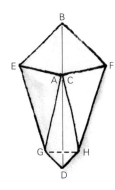

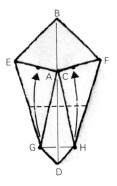

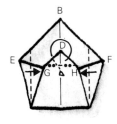

1 Using a square piece of paper, crease a diagonal line BD and unfold it. Fold corners A and C onto the crease, so that the new creases made do not quite run down to corner D.

2 Crease and unfold G to H.

3 Fold up D so that corner G lies on edge EA and corner H on CF.

4 Fold D inside, tucking it behind A and C; this locks G and H flat. Fold in E and F, butting them hard against the edges that run up to G and H.

5 Slide B under edge GH and push it until it will not go any further. Flatten and crease.

6 The complete envelope. To unlock it, pull out corner B.

Left Again, the envelopes in the photograph have been folded from a piece of paper the same size as the pieces on which they are lying.

STATIONERY HOLDER

This design can be made to take most sizes of writing paper and notecards.

Measure the stationery and add ¾ in (2 cm) to the length and the width; these two measurements will determine the size of the boards. Cut two boards to size, making sure that the corners are square and that the grain runs from top to bottom, see page 9. To allow for turn-ins, covering materials should overlap all edges by ½ in (1 cm), unless otherwise stated. Lining materials should be ½ in (12 mm) smaller than the overall measurements of the board. Draw a line down one side of the board one-fifth of the overall width. Mark this with a pair of compasses or dividers and also mark the corner on the diagonal. Repeat for the other board. (See Fig 1.)

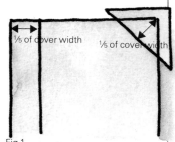

¹⁄₅ of cover width   ¹⁄₅ of cover width

Fig 1

1 Cut the bookcloth to size – twice as wide as the marked line plus at least ¾ in (2 cm) to accommodate the contents, and as long as the boards plus turn-ins. Cut a lining piece – remember constants.

2 To cut cloth for the corners use a scrap of paper along the marked line and add ½ in (1 cm) to overlap the edges, see Fig 1. Measure the square edges and cut two squares of book cloth. Cut across them diagonally to make triangles to cover the corners.

3 Brush glue onto the wrong side of the bookcloth cut for the spine – the glue should be the consistency of thick cream. Using a firm brush and scrap paper, work the glue from the centre of the piece out towards and over the edges onto the scrap.

4 Position the spine on the boards between the marked lines and turn over the edges using a bone folder or clean fingers.

5 Glue the lining strip in position and, using the bone folder, press the bookcloth well to form a groove; start from one side and work across.

6 Mark the position of the triangular piece and trim off the corner.

7 Glue the piece into position on the diagonal line and press it towards the corner. Turn over and, using the bone folder, press the edge down and work the mitre neatly into boards. Finally bring the second edge over and press it down. Repeat for the other three corners.

8 Now, mark the covering material, remembering to add extra for the turn-ins on the edges and slightly overlapping the book cloth at the spine. Position the covering material on the board and, holding it down firmly, fold back one corner so that it just covers the book cloth triangle, and crease. Repeat for the other corner. Remove from the board and trim away the corners at the folded crease.

9 Before glueing mark the position on the wrong side.

10 Work quickly, because the covering material may curl when moistened with glue.

11 Place the glued piece on the board and cover it with a piece of scrap paper. Smooth it over gently with the bone folder to remove any air bubbles. The scrap paper protects the covering material from becoming shiny with rubbing.

12 Now turn in the edges neatly, adding more glue if necessary.

13 If you want ribbon ties attach them at this stage. Cut two lengths of about 12 in (30 cm). Using a knife or chisel, cut a hole the width of the ribbon in the centre of both boards ½ in (1 cm) from the side edge.

14 Push the ribbons through these holes and glue them in place. Cover the right side with a scrap of board and hammer it to close and flatten the incision (this step is not essential).

ALTERNATIVES

If bookcloth is not available, it is possible to make your own by laminating cloth material to paper. Brush a thin layer of glue onto lightweight paper and smooth the paper carefully onto the cloth. Cover it with scrap paper and smooth it gently all over with a bone folder or the side of your hand to remove the air bubbles. Allow it to dry under weights – a pile of books or something similar.

LINING

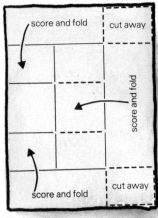

Fig 2

1 Position the lefthand lining on the righthand lining paper so that the lefthand edges are together and the excess equal at top and bottom. Using the lefthand lining as a guide, score the righthand lining paper right across the top and bottom and down the side. Trim away the top and bottom righthand rectangles. Score a second line ¼ in (6 mm) from the previous scores towards the outside edge of all three flaps. Crease and fold in – the paper now appears the same size as the board minus the lining constants, and is ready to glue into position.

To line the folder there is a variety of possibilities: you could line the righthand board with plain paper with flaps to protect the contents of the holder and to stop them falling out; you could line the lefthand board quite simply with a piece of plain paper glued in place or it could have a pocket attached for envelopes; the pocket could be made of decorative paper or it could be a different shape – see the photograph of the finished project.

For the righthand lining, cut a piece of paper 1½ times as wide and 1½ times as long as the boards, with the grain running from top to bottom, see Fig 2. For the lefthand lining, cut one piece the same size as the boards, less the constants for lining. For the pocket, cut one piece half the length of the board and the full width plus 1 in (2.5 cm).

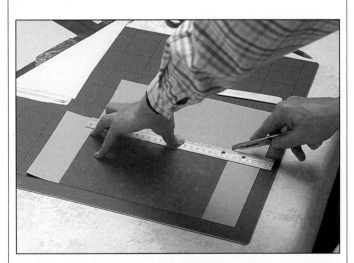

2 Score the paper cut for the pocket, using a ruler and a bone folder, ½ in (1 cm) in from the top and bottom edges. Fold and glue down one edge. This is to strengthen the top edge of the pocket. Place the pocket on the lefthand lining paper so that it overlaps equally at both sides. Score and fold in these edges.

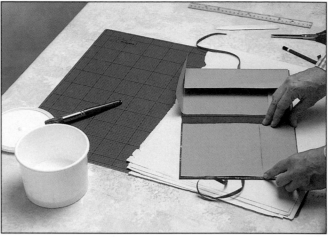

3 Trim away the double fold of the pocket as a mitre to reduce bulk. Taper, very slightly, the lower side edges of the lining for the same reason.

4 Glue the folded flaps of the pocket to the lining paper. Then glue the whole piece into position on the lefthand board.

TABLE DECORATIONS

SERVIETTE FOLDS

The use of paper as a means of table decoration is often forgotten. Most people take paper and its many uses for granted and, although paper serviettes are used each day, it is seldom that one thinks of folding them decoratively or of using a little imagination to make simple place name cards or serviette rings. Using the ideas found in this chapter, it is easy to draw together the whole table setting. Make a theme for the whole setting by choosing a colour, perhaps picked out from the dinner service or table cloth, or use a topic to suit the season.

SAIL SERVIETTE

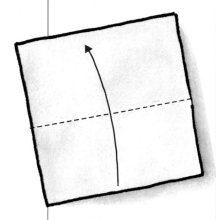

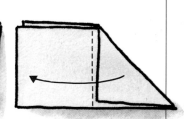

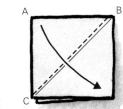

1 Fold the bottom edge up to the top.

2 Fold down the top righthand corner.

3 Fold the bottom right corner across to the left edge.

4 Fold corner A downwards. Note B and C.

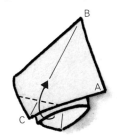

5 Open corner C, flattening the crease BC.

6 Fold up the tip of corner C . . .

7 . . . to lock and complete the sail serviette.

Right This is a simple, attractive serviette, quick to make and easy to unfold.

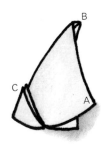

FLAME SERVIETTE

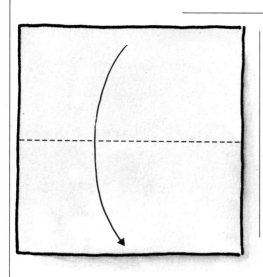

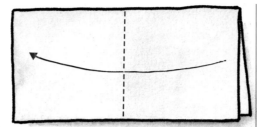

1 Fold the top edge down to the bottom.

2 Fold the righthand edge over to the left.

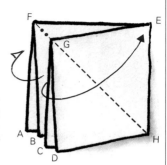

3 Look carefully at the lettered corners. Fold A and B behind to touch E and fold C and D to the front to also touch E. Crease FH and GH . . .

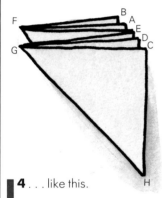

4 . . . like this.

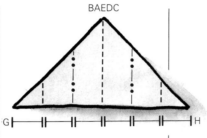

5 Pleat the triangle into six equal divisions, to look . . .

6 . . . like this.

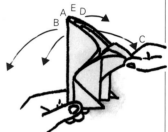

7 Hold the serviette firmly at the bottom. There are five layers of corners at the top. Tug corner C as shown, pulling it as far out as possible. Do the same with corner D next to it, but not pulling it as far. Repeat on the other side, pulling B further than A.

8 The flame serviette is complete. To hold its shape, the design needs to be placed in a wine glass or tumbler.

Left This fold is more complex than the previous one, but makes a spectacular display. Fold two together of different colours for extra visual effect.

SERVIETTE RING

EQUIPMENT

- Paper or card
- Materials to decorate the paper
- Card for template
- Pencil
- Ruler
- Knife or a pair of scissors

A good size for the ring is 6 in (15 cm) by 1 in (2.5 cm) plus ½ in (1 cm) at each end for the slit, which will be cut half-way at each end – see Fig 1. It is quite important that the grain of the paper runs in the direction of the arrow, so that it will curve easily. If you are making a curved centre (see Fig 2) it is advisable to make a template of the shape from card (see Fig 3) – this saves you drawing each one separately.

Having drawn the shape, cut it out using a knife or scissors, slide the slits together and pass the serviette through the ring, see Fig 4.

Fig 3

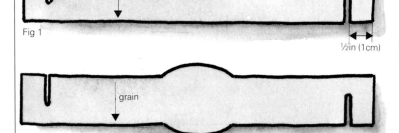

½in (1cm)

6½in (16.5cm)

grain

Fig 1

½in (1cm)

grain

Fig 2

Fig 4

Below This very simple idea can be kept quite basic and unadorned or can be decorated with many of the methods already described. For example, you could attach a miniature origami butterfly, see pages 62–3, or a small paper flower, see pages 121–4. You could use a piece of marbled paper in the chosen colour scheme, see pages 46–50, or write a name or initial on the ring to serve as a place name.

PLACE NAME CARDS

EQUIPMENT

■ Lightweight to mediumweight card
■ Card for templates
■ Paper for decorations (foil, crêpe, etc.)
■ A cocktail stick or straw
■ Glue and adhesive tape
■ Pencil and ruler
■ Knife or a pair of scissors

As with other items in this chapter, the place name cards can be quite plain or very decorative. Folding ones, which stand up on the table, look more professional and are usually easier to read.

The names can be written with a coloured pen or silver or gold markers as well as ordinary ink. The size of the card can vary a little depending on your handwriting and the length of the name, but 3–3½ in (7.5–8.5 cm) by 1¼–1½ in (3–4 cm) should allow sufficient room.

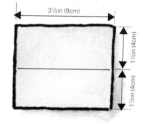

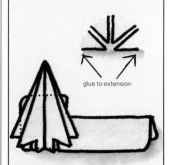

■ **Above** If one side is cut shorter than the other, the angle of the card on the table will be flatter. Draw, cut and score these cards. Then decorate them with stickers, stencil patterns, etc. Write the name on the card before folding and placing it in position.

■ **Above** Here a simple name card is illustrated.

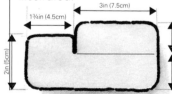

■ **Below** The extension could have other shapes glued to it to suit another season. It could also have quilled shapes, see pages 93–4, glued to it or a miniature origami design, see pages 58–74.

■ **Left** This place name card is an adaptation of the basic card.

see pages 93–4; see pages 58–74.

CHRISTMAS TREE DESIGN

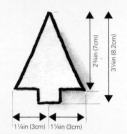

■ **1** For a Christmas tree design you will need four of these shapes; cut them from any lightweight decorative paper. Fold each shape in half.

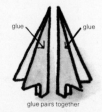

■ **2** Glue the folded halves to each other leaving two folded halves free.

■ **3** Glue the two free folded halves (see inset) to the side extension of the name card.

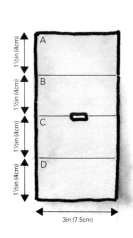

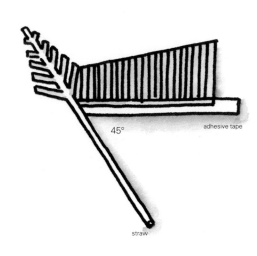

1 For the name card part of this decoration, mark a piece of card as above. Cut out the card, score and fold it and then glue section D under section A.

2 To make the tree use very lightweight paper. Cut out the shaped piece and attach adhesive tape along the straight uncut edge. The slits should be ⅛ in (3 mm) apart.

3 Take a drinking straw and, holding it at an angle of 45°, roll the adhesive tape around the straw, starting from the narrow end. The slits will fall into a tree shape. Slip the straw through the hole in the top of the card, cut it to size and then, if necessary, secure it through the base with a pin so that the tree stands upright.

Left It is possible to wrap the shaped and slit piece around the straw at an angle of 30°. This will result in a less bushy tree with a wider shape (**far left**). If you prefer this shape, wrap the straw with a strip of paper before winding the shaped piece around because the increased angle means that the straw will not otherwise be covered. Also the initial piece can be reduced in length by at least 2 in (5 cm). You could attach a miniature carnation, see pages 121–2, to a drinking straw or cocktail stick and use it in the same way. Cut leaves from suitable paper and attach them to the stem, which could be covered with stem tape or painted green.

EQUIPMENT

- Stub wire (available as for carnations)
- Stem tape (available as for carnations)
- Florist's wire
- Double-sided crêpe paper
- Pencil
- A pair of scissors
- Blunt knife

ROSES

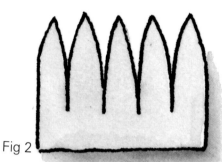

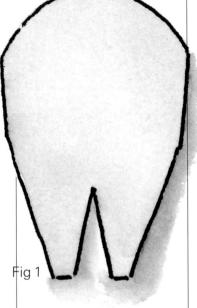

Fig 2

▌**Above** Sepal template – see step 6.

▌**Right** Petal template – see step 1.

Fig 1

▌**1** Place the petal template (see Fig 1) on the double-sided crêpe paper and fold it over so that there are nine petals, or measure a strip approximately 18½ in (47 cm) and pleat it. Cut out the petal shape, making sure that the sides remain joined. Unfold and cut off three petals.

▌**2** Decide which colour should be on the outside of the petals and work with the other colour facing you. Using a blunt knife or the back of the scissors, curl the petal tops by placing the blade behind the petal and gently but firmly drawing the crêpe paper over the blade.

▌**3** Having curled all the petal tops, cup them in the centre by stretching each petal widthways with your thumbs.

4 Take a stub wire and thread it through the petals at one end and turn it over to secure.

5 Now roll the first petal tightly around the wire. Ease the remaining five petals gently into shape — closed or open — and secure them by wrapping them with florist's wire. Twist the ends and bend them down.

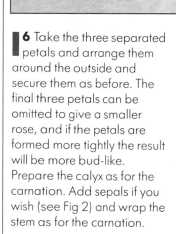

6 Take the three separated petals and arrange them around the outside and secure them as before. The final three petals can be omitted to give a smaller rose, and if the petals are formed more tightly the result will be more bud-like. Prepare the calyx as for the carnation. Add sepals if you wish (see Fig 2) and wrap the stem as for the carnation.

Right Again, use various colours of crêpe paper for a truly marvellous and realistic bouquet of flowers.

HISTORY OF PAPER

The dictionary definition of paper is a substance made from cellulose fibres derived from rags, wood or straw often with other additives, and formed into thin, flat sheets. The word is derived from the Latin word papyrus, meaning a reed.

More than 5,000 years ago the Egyptians used these reeds, cross-woven into a mat and pounded into thin, hard sheets. However, it was a Chinese man named Ts'ai Lun, who, in AD 105, invented paper as we know it today.

There is evidence of papermaking in Japan around AD 610. The Japanese used mulberry bark and developed cottage industries in papermaking which continue to this day.

In AD 751 the Arabs captured some Chinese prisoners at Samarkand and forced them to teach them the papermaking process. The paper the Arabs produced consequently was made with linen rags. It is known that there was a papermaking factory in Baghdad in AD 793 with Chinese workmen. From this time onwards the craft spread westwards, and when the Moors invaded Spain they introduced papermaking on a larger scale.

The earliest reference to an English paper mill is in a book printed by Caxton in about 1490. The mill belonged to John Tate of Hertfordshire and the paper was used for an edition of Chaucer's *Canterbury Tales*. Several more mills were recorded over the next 100 years but were not very successful; one reason that has been suggested is that papermakers were thought to help spread the plague by using discarded rags infected with disease.

The first known American paper mill was established at Germantown, Pennsylvania, in 1690. It used the European rag method. However, rags were becoming increasingly scarce and with the Industrial Revolution this problem became worse. As paper was still handmade, output was low, but there was an increasing demand for paper — books for the educated classes and for the poorer classes, who were beginning to be educated by charitable bodies and the Church; account books for the growing export trade; and daily newspapers were introduced at the beginning of the 18th century.

Seeing a need for machinery, Louis Robert, a clerk in a French mill, invented a crude papermaking machine in 1799. A model of this can be seen in the Science Museum in London. This particular machine was not very successful, but was used as the basis for an improved machine. This venture was funded by brothers Henry and Sealy Fourdrinier and developed by an engineer, Bryan Donkin. After many trials and much expense the machine was finished in 1803 and erected at Frogmore in Hertfordshire. Due to the great cost involved in developing this machine, the brothers lost a fortune, but the name of Fourdrinier lives on in the basic principles still in use today.

Paper mills today use wood pulp or recycled paper. In the United Kingdom approximately 50 per cent of the paper produced is made from recycled paper because it has no major forest resources as there are in the United States and Scandinavia. Wood pulp comes from lumber waste and from trees, which are being constantly replaced, often by fast-growing conifers. One averaged-sized tree is needed to make sufficient paper for 400 copies of a 40-page tabloid newspaper. There are three methods of extracting wood pulp: chemical, mechanical and semi-chemical. Combinations of these pulps are sometimes used, depending on the use of the finished product.

Paper mills are extremely efficient users of energy. They produce electricity, and in the United Kingdom are the second largest private generator — steam drying of the moist paper is one way in which electricity is generated. Water is also recycled during the papermaking process. One million cubic metres (metric tonnes) of water are used daily in paper manufacture — 34 per cent for processing and 66 per cent for cooling. All the cooling water is returned to source and the process water is treated and either discharged or re-used.

Some papers are still made by hand today, but the craft is not widely practised; the papers that are produced are specialist papers and costly. The mechanical papermaking industry continues worldwide and is constantly improving its techniques.

INDEX

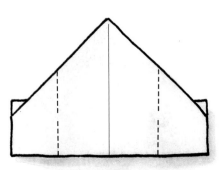